MEMORIES

OF

MADISON RUN

MEMORIES

OF

MADISON RUN

Gary Hogsten

Writers Club Press
New York Lincoln Shanghai

Memories of Madison Run

Writers Club Press
an imprint of iUniverse, Inc.

For information address:
iUniverse
2021 Pine Lake Road, Suite 100
Lincoln, NE 68512
www.iuniverse.com

Cover photo by Mark Burton.

ISBN: 0-595-26539-1

Printed in the United States of America

To Grandma Rosa, who will always be in my heart, and to all of my other kinfolk of blood and kinfolk of community, saints and sinners alike, who are set to memory from days gone by.

From Grandma Rosa came the roots of my values, both spiritual and moral. One of the lessons she taught us that has always stood out in my mind was a paraphrase of 1 Corinthians 15:33. Grandma would point with slightly curved finger to me and Ronnie, and then to Heaven, saying "Mark my words, evil communications corrupt good morals." I don't remember the specific occasions or circumstances, but the memory remains vivid.

CONTENTS

ACKNOWLEDGMENTS

Thanks to Shirley Frost, who led me to believe that someone else would actually want to read what I have written. Thanks also to Mark Burton, who worked hard and diligently to edit my manuscript and get it ready for publication. And finally, thanks to Cristy Lee for copyediting and proofreading the draft.

FOREWORD

Scattered throughout these memoirs are flashes of wit and moments of unexpected tenderness that will leave the reader yearning for the good old days of Madison Run and Orange County. With charm and warmth, Gary Hogsten captures in words Virginia's fading rural heritage, telling us what life was like growing up in a 20th century American village.

He has recorded the stories of his past in a manner not unlike a grandfather who, while sipping lemonade on the front porch, recalls at random the carefree days of his youth. In his original manuscript, Gary's friendly, anecdotal style was unconstrained by chronological or topical order. For this edition, my primary goal as editor was to improve the format and readability of the text while preserving the informality and sincerity of Gary's colloquial style. Most of my substantive additions are in the form of footnotes, which I added for clarification or background information. In three instances, I converted Gary's parenthetical remarks into footnotes, ending them with "GH" to distinguish them from mine.

It is my understanding that Gary initially intended only to produce a keepsake for his children and other loved ones to read. What he has written, however, is a touching tribute to family, friends and community that has universal appeal. He has given the world a very personal historical record of the lives and events of Madison Run, Virginia, during a century that suddenly seems, in retrospect, like another age.

Mark Burton
Gordonsville, Virginia
August 2002

PREFACE

This did not begin as an attempt to write a book because, for one thing, my spelling isn't too good and my thoughts, sentences and paragraphs kind of run together. What made me write all of this stuff was that some of us were sitting around one day telling stories about things that happened in years past. Everyone was laughing and enjoying it, so I thought that maybe the kids would like to hear them later on.

Most of this stuff was written as I remember it, but I've also added a few tales that other people have told me. A lot of the tales are funny now but, at the time they actually happened, some of them were sad, frightening or downright painful. I have tried to include just the funny stuff, but I guess some things are kind of thoughtful.

Uncle Willie Bowers impressed me as probably the best storyteller ever. His excitement, enthusiasm, laughter and knee-slapping just added so much color to his tales that we could have sat and listened to him for hours. It was a big let-down when the evening was over. Uncle Willie died in 1975 at the age of 91, so he had a lot of years to build up memories and tell stories about the old days.

I'm no match for Uncle Willie when it comes to telling stories about the old days. Of course, writing stuff on a piece of blank white paper won't ever take the place of sitting around with a bunch of people whooping and laughing at each others' fond memories of days gone by, but I guess it's better than nothing.

INTRODUCTION

Madison Run. M-a-d-i-s-o-n R-u-n. I say it twice and slow down on the second one to savor the sound and bring back the memories that touch my heart with sadness, happiness and a feeling of belonging to a time and place that I love. If there is a story of how Madison Run got its name, I've never heard it. The most plausible explanation is that a creek runs down around the outskirts that could have been called a run and James Madison lived just over Chicken Mountain. Or, possibly, the train depot was named Madison Run, because the C&O had a run to Madison or something. I don't guess it really matters, but it would be interesting to find out.

This place called Madison Run lies 3 miles south of the town of Orange, 4 miles north of Gordonsville, 2 miles east (as the crow flies) of Montpelier (the home of President James Madison) and 3 miles west of Mallory's Ford on Route 639 (where we used to go with Daddy to wash the car).

I never really thought anything about the "Run" until one day in elementary school. A boy in my class found out where I lived and said with a look of fright and awe, "You're from Madison Run?" At that time in my life, I really didn't give my place of birth and home much thought. Until that moment, I never heard or knew that the "Run" had a reputation for some rough, drunken, cussing, fighting men. I knew some of the men who had the reputation for all this activity but, by this time, they were too old to do anything but the cussin' and drinkin' part. They were pretty good-natured and an established part of the area. They are all dead now and I hope at some time or another that they made a decision to accept Christ, so that someday I'll have a chance to ask them about the fightin' part.

I can't remember anything bad about anybody that I considered a native or who, at least, had spent most of a lifetime here. For example, Carl McClendon and Alton Hall are two men whom I respect. Along with the rest of my family, well, we think the world of 'em. Lula (aka "Lulu") Hutchins is probably the newest "almost" native. She is my mother-in-law and a fine Christian lady who I think is really special. In 32 years of marriage to her daughter Jackie, this lady and I have not—and this is no lie or exaggeration—had a cross word.

I cannot say the same for me and her daughter. I just wouldn't feel right if we didn't fuss at least once a week!

I know that strangers or "outsiders" wonder why anyone would want to live here. There are some empty houses, some run-down houses and even some nice houses, but the thing of it is, it's home. Madison Run is in a beautiful part of the world and the surrounding hills are very scenic. The railroad runs smack dab through the middle and on both sides of the tracks lie the houses, yards, fields and woodlands of home. This place is fresh and beautiful in the spring, when the fields are all shades of green and when the flowers are blooming and the leaves are starting to come out on the trees. It smells wonderful in the summer after the afternoon rain has settled the dust on the dirt roads. The colors in fall are beyond imagination or artistic rendering. And in winter, when it snows, there is no place on earth like it. These hills and fields make you feel glad to be alive and to be a witness to this creation that only God could render.

Probably the most notable historical event I can mention is that the Confederate Army, led by Stonewall Jackson, camped here and two Confederate soldiers were buried in what became my parents' front yard. (The graves were later moved.) A sign on nearby Route 15 says

"Campaign of Second Manassas." Near here Stonewall Jackson camped from August 13th to 15th, 1862, after the Battle of Cedar Mountain.

Some of my cousins who moved away are reluctant to admit that they hail from these parts, which I really don't fully understand. I've always been proud to be from Madison Run and, in later years, I've become even more proud of my roots. Sure, there are places I'd like to see and places I'd like to visit, but there's only one place I want to live and that's Madison Run.

Probably the next most notable thing that happened in Madison Run was when Junior Atkins welded together four towers, with winged aircraft models on two towers and spacecraft models on the other two. Then he cut Columbus' three ships out of steel and welded them to the fence at the gated entrance to his property. The gate posts have big globes on them that represent the earth and some other things that have historical significance. These things may not be to everyone's taste, but they have been there quite a few years now and are sort of a landmark. I hope that they will remain and that kids will continue to marvel at them for years to come.

Junior and his wife Edith may be considered eccentric. You always see them in the old blue truck or on the tractor. One thing is, when you see Junior, you see Edith, and when you see Edith, you see Junior. Just like two peas in a pod, they stick together and kind of stick to themselves.

I have fond memories of growing up in Madison Run. We had small troubles and others had small troubles but, all in all, most of us respected and loved each other. People in the community called their elders "uncle" and "aunt" whether they were cousins or not kin at all. In our youth, if someone lived pretty close, we considered them actual kin and a lot of time, they were. Just to name a few, we had Uncle Mutt, Aunt Minnie, Uncle Albert, Aunt Hester, Uncle Harry, Aunt Lovell, Uncle Nat, Aunt Nat, Aunt Wilmeta, Uncle Raymond, Uncle Walker, Aunt Freda, Uncle Sam, Aunt Thomasia, Aunt Annie, Aunt Virginia and many, many more. I suppose that we really were kin in some way, but the exact lineage didn't matter; they were our aunts and uncles and were referred to as such out of respect.

All of these folks are dead now. It seems that the old folks slip away one at a time, and then it dawns on us that they are all gone. We forgot to ask them things that we wonder about now, and we didn't take time to tell them the things that we wish we had. And then we just miss them.

Then the realization dawns on us that *we* are the old folks now. Well, almost.

Now Grandpop and Grandma are fond memories. I don't remember a lot about Grandpop; he died in 1947. I do remember that he had a kind face. When he died, Mama made me and my older brother Ronnie kiss his forehead. I remember going fishing one day and a whipporwill was calling down by the creek. I was not quite five years old but this has always been vivid in my mind. The very next day, while we were watching a Mickey Mouse movie at the Orange Theater, Grandpop died. He and Ronnie had been good buddies.

Grandma died in 1956 after a long illness. This was hard on Mama because she had to work at the American Silk Mill in Orange and look after Grandma all night. Ronnie and I weren't much help because we couldn't keep awake. Then Uncle Woodson (he really was our uncle) died. I thought a lot of him. Then Rick (our real cousin) was killed in an automobile accident. Rick was like a brother, we thought so much of him. Then Aunt Fannie Mae (our real aunt) died. Everyone loved her.

Daddy died in 1988. He was a tough man who was small in stature but big in guts and heart. He tried to do a lot more than most people thought that he could do. In fact, if Daddy set out to do something, he did it. Daddy did woodwork—refinishing antique furniture mostly, for which he never charged enough. He was a barber who had the reputation of being the best around; was a pioneer in doing flat tops; even built his own cinder block workshop—all after being partially paralyzed in 1945 by a tumor on his spine at the back of his neck.

Most people in his condition would have given up and taken welfare or disability, but not Daddy. He worked every day until he was 72. Daddy said that when he was in the hospital, packed in sandbags to keep his spine straight, the doctors thought that he was dying and called the family back for a last good-bye. Daddy said that he was lying there in great pain with great beads of sweat on his face. Mama and the rest were looking down at him and mourning because of his impending death. Although Daddy couldn't speak, he thought to himself, "You're crying for the wrong man. I'm not leaving here yet."

He didn't. He lasted another 43 years.

Daddy made a lot of friends at the barber shop. A lot of people knew him. He was a familiar figure, swinging that right leg when crossing the street to the barber shop, with cane in hand. He wasn't perfect; like anyone else, he had his faults. But I have to give him a lot of credit for teaching Ronnie and I to be decent children and adults: to not be quitters, to not use bad language and to try to do things right. And he taught us not to be wasteful—it would be a big fault if we were.

I was proud of my Daddy. He suffered a lot of pain and disability in his life, but he was not a quitter. Not too long before he died, I told him that I was proud of him and I'm truly glad that I did. Eventually, Daddy was in such pain that we took him to the hospital, where he later died. I know that he would rather have been sitting in his old black chair in the corner when he went to be with the Lord, but we couldn't bear to see him suffer any longer without proper medical attention.

Mama was, in my eyes, the greatest mother in the world. After all, she went through 9 months of carrying me and another 19 years of worrying about me driving a car, staying out late and being with the wrong crowd. She was a proud woman who had to work hard for a living. I always thought that she should have had a lot of money, with maids to do the housework and cooking. Instead, she worked eight hours a day, raised Ronnie and me, took care of Grandma and, when Daddy got sick, she had to look after him. Mama really looked forward to the time she could retire, which she did at age 64. Daddy got really down right after she retired and she had to take care of him most of the time. So after he died, she finally had the time to do some of the things she had always wanted to do, like travel. By that time, though, the people who would have gone with her had also died.

Sometimes I think that not being tied down, being free to do what she wanted, was more important than actually doing those things. Well, she did get to take a trip to California before Daddy got in bad shape. Jack and Estelle Chandler (her cousin) drove out to California and invited her along. And Mama always had some old people that she would visit, take to the store or help with whatever they needed. That was about all the other traveling she did.

When we were small, Mama always saw that we got what we needed and more. Especially at Christmas time. This was a big thing for Ronnie and me, and for her, too. I remember us sitting for hours coloring strips of notebook paper to make chains (glued together with flour paste) to crisscross the parlor ceiling. She always tried to get us matching gifts, except one time Ronnie got a Daisy Defender BB gun and I got an erector set.

What I really wanted was a chemistry set. Shucks, what can you blow up with an erector set? I eventually got a chemistry set but it wasn't much good for anything exciting, although it did make a pretty respectable stink bomb. One year we both got black cowboy suits with chrome pistols and black 10-gallon hats. We really felt tough. Then we both got brand new bicycles—I mean 26-inch bikes that I know she had to scrimp to save the money to buy. Christmas was a happy time.

I almost forgot: another time we got real Davy Crockett coonskin caps. I mean these were real skin—even had the coon's face skinned and sewn to the front of the cap with eyes as big as nickels that glowed in the dark.

Mamas have a special place in the heart. When you are young, and especially when you are getting to be teenager, you tend to think that they are just trying to keep you from having fun or that they are just being mean. Then you have children of your own and you realize that your parents just wanted you to be safe, to stay out of trouble and not get involved with the wrong activities or the wrong people. I have told my children, when they get mad at their mom, that "no one on earth will ever love you as much or any more than your mom, even when she is on the warpath." I remember one time, when I was 15 or 16, I said a curse word to Mom. She probably forgot about it, but I never will.

Some years back, I started some remodeling at Mama's house. It was a way I could show her that I loved and cared for her and wanted her to have a house that she could be proud of. I must say, it was a pretty good job for a rank amateur. That old house meant a lot to Mama and it still means a lot to me and Ronnie and our families. It is what we would call our roots. Ronnie and I both were born in the house, as were Mama, Annalee and Rosalee. Not many people can sleep in the same bed, in the same room, that they were born in more than 50 years earlier.

Mama's house had a parlor that, in the past, was used to lay out people for viewing when they died. When I was little, we used to step by the parlor door real fast, especially if the door was open. We didn't know who or what might be in that room. I heard that Annalee, Rosalee, Jack, Aileen and Tommy didn't hang around the door too long either, especially at night. (They are first cousins and older than Ronnie and me by about 20 years.) To tell the truth, when it's dark and I go by that room now, the hair on the back of my neck rises up. So I'll turn the light on and look in just to prove to myself that I'm an adult and that things like that are just for kids. But when Annalee and Rosalee come down to visit now, they still don't linger around the old parlor door.

Mama taught us to work hard by example. She never missed work and was always on time. Now I don't ever miss a scheduled work day and Ronnie is the same way. She taught us to go to church and to say our prayers at night. All in all, I love my Mama and I guess most people love theirs, too. I tend to think that if you don't love your Mama, how in the world could you love anybody else, even the Lord for that matter?

I am so lucky that the Lord blessed me with a wife that loves my family. My wife Jackie truly loved both my Mama and Daddy, and this means a lot to me. She always went above and beyond the call of duty as a daughter-in-law by making doctor appointments for them and then making sure that they went. She would pick them up and take them, even when she had a lot of other stuff to do. You hear about in-laws feuding and fighting, and I wonder why. I guess I wonder because I have never experienced such behavior. Jackie also shows sisterly love to Ronnie and his wife, Darnita, and I am thankful that we have a good all-around family relationship. We've had some truly great times going places to sing together and to vacation together. Darnita is always wrong and I'm always right, although she won't admit it. But she still can't help but love me like a brother, and I her, like a sister.

On those occasions when Darnita happens to agree with me, which is very seldom, it causes me to think, "Well, maybe I'm wrong." All good naturedly, of course. When we go to sing together, Darnita sometimes introduces me as her little, fat brother-in-law. I admit that I am pretty good sized. I'm also kind of shy, so it is really nice to have someone like Darnita to stand in front of me so people can't see me while we are singing....

Anyway, I love my wife. After all, how could I not love someone who loves me, loves my family and loves the Lord? She's concerned about most people, is the mother of my children, and has stuck with me for more than 35 years. I told her the other day that if she died before I did, I wouldn't get married again. After all, how could I replace a part of me? If we can make it through her hot flashes, it's clear sailing.

At one time or another, all of us have had and still have problems, sorrows, anger and minor regrets. But as a whole, I would not change a thing about my life, except maybe sassing Grandma and saying that curse word to Mama.

Speaking of sorrows, Daddy was in such misery before he died that I can't feel a total loss about his passing. In other words, I'm thankful that his suffering is over and that he is in a place with no disabilities. We miss Mama, too, but I am thankful that the Lord took her without her having to go through the infirmities of old age. One of her worst fears was having to go into a nursing home and not being able to take care of herself. We would not have allowed that to happen, anyway. She died in the place that she loved most—home. I can almost see her playing the piano for a choir of angels.

I don't know if there are such things as premonitions but, about two weeks before she died, Mama went to visit Annalee and Rosalee in Maryland for Thanksgiving. The whole time, whenever I went by her house, I would get this feeling of sorrow that I had never had before. The day after she got home, she thanked me for watching the house and keeping the fires burning, and she hugged my waist and I kissed her forehead. Ten minutes later she was gone to a greater reward.

That big, old white house, with the double porches on the front, sitting on the northeast corner of Madison Run, means a lot to me, Jackie and the kids. Ronnie probably feels the same way. That's where the memories are stored of Grandma, Grandpop, Mama, Daddy and all of the aunts, uncles, cousins, friends and relations by association. The good times that I remember outweigh the bad so heavily that it is hard to remember anything bad at all. I could leave the old place standing as is. To have someone else live there would be sort of like having strangers live in Monticello, Montpelier or Mount Vernon. After all, those people were no better, nor do they deserve any more honor, than my relatives. I know that this sounds a little far out of center, but that's how I feel about it.

THE
CHILDHOOD YEARS

The reason that I'm writing all of this is because I'm a sentimental person. I see nothing wrong with reflecting on the past, as long as you don't get in a rut that hinders progress or keeps you from reality. I would love to sit down and read what my ancestors had written about their past and their present. What I really meant to write about, though, were some of the funny things that Ronnie, I and our friends and relatives did as kids. But I kind of got off track.

My first "almost" mishap in life occurred when I was almost born in the thunder jug.[1] Maybe I shouldn't admit to this but, in any case, there it is, the true fact. On top of that, Dr. Scott was called but he was a little slow getting started, so someone called him back.

He replied, "What's wrong with you people? Are you crazy?"

That might be the case, but little Gary (that's me) arrived before Dr. Scott did. While little me was protesting vocally my entrance into this cold world, Mama was wailing "He's going to die!"

Grandma, being a very positive person, responded, "Shuh, anything making that much fuss sure isn't going to die."

So far, so good.

---

[1] Probably a local variation of "thunder mug," a 19th century slang term for chamber pot. —*Ed.*

The Adventures Begin

The first ornery thing that I remember doing (and knowing better) was pushing the tricycle off of the porch and breaking its handle bars. Aunt Fannie Mae, however, knew how to get me and Ronnie straightened out if we got too rowdy. She would get out the old upright, bagger vacuum cleaner. When she turned that thing on and it started to scream and whine, we were both too terrified to do anything but cower on the sofa. It got to the point that all she had to do was put her hand on the closet doorknob and we became instant little angels.

When we lived in Baltimore for a short period, there was a little boy who would borrow my trike and ride way off down the street, far enough that he never could make it back in time to go to the bathroom. Needless to say, I ended up with a messy seat. To add insult to injury, I'm the one who had to go get his mother to clean it off, even though I was only 4 or 5 years old. It embarrassed me to do it.

Then there was Ricky. He was a cousin who was a little younger than I. He must have thought I was made of hamburger or something, given the way he used to bite and gnaw on me all of the time. (He had to have his teeth straightened out when he got older.) One time, Daddy got mad and made me bite him back, but not very hard, just to make him stop biting me.

One time when we (when I say "we," I mean my brother Ronnie and I) were left alone for a while, a little incident occurred for which I don't think we should bear all of the blame. After all, someone else left the bottle of Mercurochrome laying around where two artistic little boys could find it.[2] Well, it just so happened that there were some black and white baby pictures of me and Ronnie that looked awful plain and drab and could do with a bit of touching up. A few finessed strokes with that

---

[2] Mercurochrome is or was a trademark brand of merbromin, a mercurial compound in a red solution used as a local antiseptic and germicide. —Ed.

Mercurochrome dauber across the cheeks, in our opinion, really set those pictures off. Rosy cheeks on babies always look nice. Having done so well on the baby pictures, we decided that the velvet picture of Jesus praying in the garden could use a little improvement. Mama appreciated our art work so much that she gave us one of her superior switchings. On a scale of 1 to 10, I would rate it a 12.

Back in first grade at the old Gordonsville Elementary School, all of the kids sat around tables, boys and girls together. Our table had me, Peter, Puggy, Simon, Reggie, Cecil and Eddie sitting along with some girls. One day, Puggy dropped his pencil and it rolled under the table. So he crawled under to get it and discovered that he could see under the girls' dresses. He got back to his seat and told the rest of us about it. Naturally, throughout the rest of the day, pencils got awfully slippery. There wasn't anything sexual about this; it was just mischievousness. It was a wonder, though, that Miss Fitzhugh didn't notice.

On another day at Gordonsville Elementary, I had a major crisis. I was headed for the bus to go home when this big, older, red-headed boy stepped in front of me and said, "I'm going to beat you up."

Now this old boy went around beating up on smaller kids. Since I was only in the fourth grade and he was in the sixth or seventh, there was a good bit of difference between his size and mine. He looked huge and I was scared. He was standing with his hands on his hips, scowling, with his chin jutted out, and I could see that the end was near. Since he was between me and the bus, it looked like my chances of escape were minimal to none, so I figured "What have I got to lose?"

I balled my fist up and, with all my strength, let him have it in the solar plexis. Then I ran for the bus. I mean I was smoking pavement. I rolled up on that old bus, fully expecting to get nailed from behind any second. But, glory be, I was alone. Looking out the bus window, I saw him lying on the ground, holding his stomach. Just before the bus left, Red came up to the bus window, holding his stomach with one hand and shaking the other fist at me.

"I'm going to get you," he threatened.

I truly thought that he would, until several days later. On a trip to the restroom by myself, who should walk in but old Red. By the way, to get to the restroom, you had to go outside and under the building. Boy, was I in trouble—out of earshot with no one to help me. But, you know, he just said "hello" and went on. I must have earned his respect with that one, fearful, desperate blow!

Cousins

When I was little, I had a hero who happened to be my first cousin on my Daddy's side. His name was Marvin and Uncle Sam and Aunt Thomasia were his parents. You hear people talk about professional athletes, but none of them could hold a candle to my cousin Marvin. In my mind, if people had known my cousin, all of those other sports stars—pro or amateur—would have meant little. I mean, just imagine having the greatest football player that had ever played at Orange High School, or anywhere else, as your first cousin.

Marvin was six or seven years older than us, so we really didn't associate with him at all. But once in a while, if Marvin was standing at his front door or in his yard, he would bless us by making faces at us as we walked past. We would go on by, thrilled that such a big time star athlete would even acknowledge that us little fellows existed. For him to take time to do that just verified his greatness. When we went to Baltimore, Washington, or Richmond, we couldn't understand why our relatives acted like they had never heard of Marvin and the Orange High Hornets. I guess they must have been pulling our legs.

One time, Marvin was coming down Dobyn's Hill on his bicycle, wide open, when some loose gravel caused him to lose control and wreck. (It was a dirt road back then.) Luckily, a man just happened to drive by at about that time. The man put Marvin into the back of his pick-up truck and took him to the doctor. That had to have been the greatest bicycle wreck that had ever happened on Dobyn's hill.

On another occasion, Marvin ran his sleigh into a pile of logs, resulting in the greatest sleigh wreck that ever happened. In my mind, if Marvin crashed, wrecked or whatever, it had to have been done in a heroic way.

One of my best little boy thrills came when we were on the back side of our regular sleigh riding hill. When I got there, who should I find but Marvin. He looked at me and said, "Let's go down."

This hill was steeper and more dangerous than our regular hill. It was steep part way, then it got even steeper. On top of that, there was a swamp and a creek at the bottom. If it had been anyone but Marvin, I wouldn't even have considered the thought of risking life and limb riding on someone's back down that hill. But with Madison Run's greatest hero, who could refuse? Certainly not me.

I remember waking up on the top porch on a summer morning and seeing Aunt Fannie Mae getting out of her car, very happy. But where were Ricky, Tim and Sally? Why didn't they come? They did. They were hiding behind the front seat. Oh, happy day! I was so happy I could have just busted. Ronnie and I really looked forward to Ricky, Tim and Sally (all cousins) coming down from Maryland to stay with us. They were actually second cousins, but we always thought of them as first cousins. Their mothers, Annalee and Rosalee (did I mention they were twins?) were 21 years older than us, so we considered them aunts until we were at least 11 or 12 years old. They are still really special and mean a lot to both my family and Ronnie's family.

We used to go to Baltimore and spend a week or two with our cousins. I really enjoyed those visits. A lot of time was spent in Annalee's basement, building model airplanes. They called me a mole because I spent so much time down there. Daddy helped me build my first airplane when I was about six years old and I've had a life-long love of model airplanes ever since. I've built block models, stick models, free flight, control line and radio control. Anything that flies interests me, with old World War II planes being my favorite.

One time when Ricky, Tim and Sally came down for a visit from Baltimore, some things happened for which we cannot take all of the blame. It seemed that city slickers thought their children needed to rest and take naps in the middle of the day for some reason. I really think it was more for the benefit of the adults than for the kids. More than likely, it gave them a little rest from all of the noise and excitement of fighting one minute, laughing the next, rocking chickens and doing things that the adults considered dangerous.

Of course, Ronnie and I were tough country boys. We thought nothing of climbing fifteen or twenty feet up in an old apple tree on limbs that were so flimsy an old possum would not hang from them by his tail, or pushing a rope swing so high that slack would come in the ropes and we would free-fall a couple of feet until the slack jerked out of the rope. And why in the world would anyone think that railroad tracks are dangerous? Any five- or six-year-old in the world has sense enough to step aside for a train to go by, especially when the engineer would blow his whistle as if he thought we didn't see him coming. I guess that if there had been a creek or pond around, Annalee and Rosalee would have chained us all to a tree to keep us from drowning.

We never could figure out why city slicker kids had to operate on a schedule. So what if we ate when we felt like it or didn't take scheduled naps or sit-down rest periods? The way we looked at it, a lot of playing time was being wasted eating, resting, napping and listening to someone hollering all the time:

"Where are you kids?"

"Stay in the yard."

"Get off the tracks!"

"Don't push so high."

"That limb is going to break…."

"Stay out of the road."

"Get off that roof!"

"Put that fire out!"

"Don't play with that butcher knife!"

With all of those rules and regulations, you would have thought that us country boys couldn't take care of ourselves when our city cousins came for a visit. Even with the nagging from the old folks, we still had a great time doing what we could get away with.

I mentioned "rocking chickens" a while back. The way you did this was to get a handful of green apples and find a flock of chickens bunched real close together. Then you would just stand back and let the apples fly. The idea was to knock out a chicken. Ronnie was always the best at this. He had an arm that would have qualified for the big leagues and he had deadly aim with any object he threw. We would also go to the chicken house after they had gone to roost and hurl green apples through the roost to knock down birds. Sometimes two would fall with one pitch. Actually, we never really hurt the birds.

Ricky was pretty fast on his feet but he wasn't too good at rocking chickens because his aim was a little off (city boy, you know). One day when the rest of us were getting into something else, we heard this big ka-boom. Ricky had knocked his chicken out that day. In fact, he wounded a couple more. If you get right down to it, of course, it was cheating. After all, anybody could hit a flock of chickens at fifty feet with a shotgun.

I also mentioned a roof a while back. This reminds me of the time that Ronnie, Ricky, Sally, Tim and myself were up on the shed roof. We were probably trying to see how close to the edge we could walk or something, or maybe we couldn't think of anything better to do than get up high and survey the surrounding countryside. Anyway, it started to rain a little bit. Everybody got down but Sally. That old roof was covered with some kind of black tar paper and when it got wet, the black rubbed off. When Sally got down she looked like a tar baby. She was a mess. One thing about Sally—she was one of the boys.

What I started to mention a while back was, who in their right minds would put five kids in a room by themselves to take a nap and leave a little stove poker laying around where we could find it? You know, that little poker made the neatest little round holes in the wall plaster you ever saw. That is, if it hit between the laths. If it hit on the wooden laths, it tended to bounce and fling off big chunks of plaster. If you think about it, then, the man who did the plastering was at fault, too. If he had put the laths a little farther apart and stuck the plaster a little tighter, we would have made more neat holes and had fewer big chunks of plaster fall off. Then again, Ricky, Tim and Sally probably instigated the whole thing. The reason I say this is because Ronnie and I were a little older and a little wiser, and most of the time stayed out of serious trouble. When I say "stay out of trouble," it means "not get caught." And there was no way that we were not going to get caught on that one.

There were many things that did not scare us very much when we were young. Cliff climbing, swinging limb-to-limb, drinking cider made from rotten apples and climbing to the top of tall barns were nothing to us. What really did scare us was the atom bomb, going to the doctor, going to the dentist and walking past that parlor door at night (with the dentist and the parlor door at the top of the list).

Speaking of fright, we loved scaring our city-slicker cousins. They were really gullible. One time, Sally, Ricky, Tim, Joe, Mike and maybe Faye and Debbie were upstairs in the big bedroom. We were out on the porch telling ghost stories to them through the window. It had gotten pretty dark and we had their undivided attention, so none of them noticed the white shirt hanging on the old gas light in the middle of the room. After we had them all primed up, we started yelling "There's a ghost behind you!" And it did look pretty ghostly, with that white shirt and the gas light globe looking like a head.

Well, you never heard such blood-curdling screaming and hollering in all your life. Uncle Thomas Groomes was the only adult there at the time. When he heard all of that commotion, he came running up the stairs yelling "What's wrong?" That scared us because we thought that stirring up Uncle Thomas would mean big trouble for us. Instead, we ended up getting away with another one.

Another time, Ricky was upstairs in our room by himself. We already had him kind of nervous with our tales, so we decided to pull another prank. We went outside, put a hat on a long pole and bumped it up against the second floor bedroom window. When Ricky heard the noise, then turned and saw that hat, he didn't bother to check to see if it had a head in it. He didn't know who or what was at that window that high off the ground, and he wasn't about to hang around to find out. I don't think Rick's feet touched anything but the first and last step on his way down the stairs, and he hollered in fright all the way. Man, oh, man, what a good laugh we had out of that.

Annalee decided that it was time to tell Rick and Tim about the birds and the bees. So, with dry mouth and sweaty palms, she sat down and began to speak. Rick and Tim said, "Gee, Mom, Ronnie and Gary already told us all about that!" Shucks, what good are country boys, if they don't share their wisdom?

Another time, we were out in the orchard just fooling around. Ronnie was chewing a little tobacco and Rick decided that he would like to try it. Well, he started to get sick, so Ronnie told him that he would have to run to get over it. So, off goes Rick, running through the orchard getting sicker and sicker all the time. When he got back, Ronnie asked, "Is the back of your throat dry? And are you dizzy and still sick?"

"Yes," Rick said.

"If you don't get a drink of water quick," Ronnie said, "you're going to die."

So off goes Rick again, this time running to a neighbor's house to beg for water. Pounding on the door, he yelled, "Please, lady, I need a drink of water. I'm dying." She convinced him that he was going to be all right, and he did quickly recover after his drink of water.

Those were some of the good old days, all right, when we looked forward to our cousins coming down for a visit. By the time a visit was over, we all would have scrapped, ganged up on each other and disagreed loudly. But when their car had pulled away, it was the saddest and loneliest feeling in the world. We even let a tear or two slip by. Of course, the car kicking up all that dust when it pulled out caused this, because country boys don't cry. We loved our cousins, and yes, those were the good old days.

Diggers

Ronnie and I never fought very much, mainly because he was much bigger and stronger, so why fight a losing battle? Now I am bigger. He probably still is stronger, but he has a sore back and an aching belly, so I guess that kind of evens us out a little bit.

Daddy should have named Ronnie "Digger" when he was born. He was always wanting to dig a hole for something, like a swimming pool, a pond or a cave. I hate to dig, but he would get started digging and say, "That's all right, buddy-o. If you don't help me, you're not going to swim in my pool." So, despite a lack of enthusiasm, I would pitch in.

Most of the time the ground would be too hard or we would just get tired and lose interest. Once, though, he did get a pretty respectable hole dug down in the bottom. (The "bottom" was a low-lying area where the ground was soft.) So "Digger" started his pool and, of course, I was suckered into helping. But this hole was different. The ground was soft, we could use the dug-up dirt to make a dam, and rainwater washed down the hillside to fill it. That pool was Ronnie's greatest success as a pool engineer. It was about 12 feet across, about 15 feet long and 15 to 24 inches deep. We could actually paddle around in it. We even made a boat out of an old wooden trunk to float around in. That wasn't too bad an achievement for 9- and 10-year-olds.

Then there was the time that we got the great idea to dig a tunnel. We had had ideas about digging tunnels before, but this was the best one of all. There was a big, old carbide tank in the ground that, at one time, had been used to fuel the gas lights in the house. It was seven or eight feet deep. We figured that if we got down inside and cut a hole in the side of the tank, it would be easy to make a tunnel from that point on. So down we went with axes and hatchets. We chopped us a nice two-by-two hole in the side of that old tank. Cutting the hole in that metal was quite an accomplishment for two little boys, but I guess the greatest achievement was not cutting off each others' fingers, toes, hands, feet, heads or other body parts.

We had gotten a little tunnel started, about three or four feet into the ground, when it dawned on us that the thing could cave-in. So we laid off for a few days. Meanwhile, Uncle Woodson came down and filled in the old tank with rocks, dirt and junk. I bet if we cleaned that old tank out, we could finish that tunnel....

That makes me think of the words of a song that goes "Oh, to be a child again...." To me, childhood was the best time in life because the only thing that I had to be concerned about was what I was going to do to have fun that day, like talking Mama into taking us to the Saturday movie, or finding a nice ripe apple to eat, or finding a big patch of juicy, red strawberries along the tracks. If I could go back in time, I wouldn't want to be 30 or 20 or 16; I would just like to be a child again. But 50 isn't too bad an age, if I could just hold it here and not grow older. Of course, when I'm 60, I'll probably say the same thing.

Trains

I remember sitting on Grandma's porch and watching section gangs work on the railroad tracks. They were all black and they worked together as a team. They would chant together and, to a certain tune, they would move rails and ties with an ease made possible only by their rhythmic collaboration. And the old, black steam engines would come roaring by in a cloud of steam and smoke and cinders. Later, we thought it was great when the bright orange streamliners began coming by. These were oil-fired steam engines with a smooth shell on them. Now it's great to see an old, black steam engine come rolling by again.

We were over playing with Peter and James one day when we heard this loud explosion. Looking toward the crossing, we could see steam, dust and other things going up in the air. A man we knew as Mr. Wolfrey had pulled up on the railroad crossing in front of a speeding streamliner passenger train. Needless to say, Mr. Wolfrey was killed and his lumber truck was torn to pieces. The engine stopped right along in front of our house and you could see a lot of lumber jammed under its wheels. Another engine had to tow the damaged engine away.

Some time after that, another train stopped in front of our house one night. A man named Jimmy had been sitting on the rails drinking and must not have heard the train coming. This happened about six hundred feet up from our house. He, too, was killed. Mr. Hall worked for the railroad, so he had to go check out the accident. He was the first one on the scene and, according to him, it was a pretty bad sight—especially because the man who was killed was from the neighborhood.

Joyce

We used to go over to Aunt Hester's to play with Peter and James, but I don't think she liked it very much. I think that maybe she thought we were going to lead them astray. Maybe she was right. Peter and James claimed that they tried to hang Joyce Hicks in the hay barn one time, but Joyce says she slipped and got her head caught in the cord. Anyway, she had a terrible rope burn around her neck. I tend to lean toward believing Joyce's story, because she was a little clumsy. She couldn't ride a two-wheeler, but she could ride a sleigh pretty good—as long as it wasn't actually moving. When Joyce was on a sleigh, she was just like a bullet—the only time she turned was if she hit something and ricocheted.

One time, Joyce was barreling down a hill on a sleigh, when here comes Percy Cox in his car. I have to wonder how that sleigh, with Joyce on top, went clear under that car without Joyce getting seriously injured or even killed. Poor old Percy was all shook up. Joyce, however, figured that it was just one of those things.

I also have to wonder why anyone would want to build a fire at the bottom of a hill in the vicinity of a sleigh track. Why, someone might run her sleigh through the fire.… I wonder if Aunt Minnie got mad about Joyce's singed eyebrows and clothing?

Speaking of Joyce, one time she and William came to a little birthday party for me. We had cake, ice cream and Kool Aid served with paper plates and cups. Well, after the party was over, William and Joyce decided that they needed to take those used paper plates along with them. Since they wanted the plates, I figured that there must have been something good you could do with used paper plates. When they started off with those plates, in my frustration and ignorance, I yelled out, "I'm going to tell my grandmother on you." I didn't live that saying down for a long time.

Years later, Joyce Hicks Palmer told me about Miss Eleanor. Miss Eleanor was Joyce's great aunt. We always thought Miss Eleanor was just great. She would come out and play with us on the gravel pile once in a while. But Joyce apparently doesn't have the same fond memories that we have. It seems that she and Miss Ellie didn't get along too well. When

Miss Ellie came to visit Joyce and her family, Uncle Mutt had Miss Ellie sleep in the bed with Joyce. According to Joyce, Miss Ellie didn't like her very much. Occasionally, she went so far as to pour hot water from the tea kettle on Joyce to prove the point. Joyce said that she really didn't pay much attention to the water until it made her new dress shrink up one day.

In addition, Uncle Mutt's house had a bad place in the roof that leaked a little bit during hard rains, right over Joyce's bed. So, Uncle Mutt always made Joyce move over and let Miss Ellie sleep on the dry side. It rained one night and Miss Ellie must have been feeling extra mean. She made Joyce sleep on the dry side, just so Uncle Mutt would give Joyce a switching for being disrespectful to Miss Ellie.

Also, Miss Ellie would always sing half the night. Joyce thought that she did this to keep her awake. Aunt Ellie's favorite song, it seems, was *In the Sweet By and By*. She sang it at the top of her lungs and really dragged out the "byyyy." One night it really poured down a frog strangler. This must have suited Aunt Ellie just fine because it meant that she would have another opportunity to get Uncle Mutt to punish Joyce. Well, Miss Ellie was really tuning up with a long, drawn out rendition of *In the Sweet By and By*, when the roof gave way. A stream of water poured straight down her throat and cut that hymn off with a strangled coughing fit. Joyce gets a gleam in her eye when she tells this part of the story, like real satisfaction.

Embarrassing Moments

When we were little, we used to sit on Grandma's store porch and listen to the coon dogs hunting down in the piney woods. Some of the men could tell which dog was treeing the coon by his sound. They would say "There's old Buck" or old Jake, Blue or Blackie. I don't know how they could tell one from another; they all sounded the same to me.

One day, Ronnie, Peter, James and I, and maybe Wiggly, were riding on the back of Uncle Albert's old work horse. As we passed near the barn, the old horse must have thought that the open door looked mighty cool and inviting because, first thing we knew, he made a break for the door. Everybody ducked but Peter. Needless to say, Peter got a nice lump and a nice headache.

I probably shouldn't tell this one, but one day Ronnie and I were out by the chicken pen when one or both of us stepped in some chicken manure with our bare feet. So we said, "What the heck?" and spent the next few minutes seeing how much fresh, hot manure we could get between our toes. I think Ronnie won. His feet were bigger than mine.

Another time, some of us little boys—I think it was Ronnie, Bub, Billy and myself—were skinny-dipping in the spring where the pond is now. There we were, floating in the muddy water, stark naked, when we heard a noise. It was Goldie and her daughter Sarah. They had come to see what we were up to. We grabbed our clothes and hauled freight out of there.

I don't know why it was so embarrassing to be caught naked. When Ronnie and I were a little younger, we would do our version of the streak by running in front of Lindy and her daughter without our clothes on, just to make them holler and laugh. Lindy was a black lady who would come to help Grandma every once in a while. She was a nice lady and Grandma thought a lot of her. I never heard Grandma or anyone else in the family call black people names or speak badly about them. That set a good example for us, because now we don't, either.

One day we were playing in a storage bin on the front porch of the store when a fella came by and asked if we were comfortable. Since we had never heard that word before, he took the time to explain the definition to us while he figured out how to get to the money drawer in the store. Later that day, while Grandma, Ronnie and I were up in the yard being "comfortable," he broke into the store and made off with the cash.

He should have stuck to teaching English because he was caught the next day and spent time being "comfortable" in jail.

I also remember sitting and playing in the shade of the trees in front of the house. Grandpop had made a swing out of barrel staves and rope, and he had hung it between two big old trees. (One tree still has the hook in it.) Anyway, we got the idea that if we swung that old swing hard enough, it would go all the way around without dumping us out. Believe me, it didn't. After several attempts, we gave it up because it was just too painful. It really was a good swing, though, when used properly.

Grandma

Grandma was a kind, generous person, almost to a fault. She allowed customers to charge things from her store, knowing that she probably would never receive payment. She signed banknotes for people that she had to make good, she fed people during the Depression and she even took people in to stay for a while. She did, however, have a reputation for fussing a lot, but I don't think that she really meant any harm. She just wanted to make sure that everybody knew exactly what they had done wrong and why it should not be done again. She wanted to make double and sometimes triple sure that everyone knew exactly what she was talking about when she spoke. We use to call her, with humor and out of range of her hearing, "the war horse." You know, we never did go to reform school like Grandma predicted we would. Of course, she probably thought that all kids were a little sassy.

Another thing about Grandma was that she believed in sparkling clean ears. In my opinion, if you wanted to torture someone, all you had to do was get Grandma to wash his ears. She would wrap that old coarse rag around her finger, clinch her tongue between her teeth in the corner of her mouth, and go for the dirt and wax. I wondered how she thought her finger, with that rag wrapped around it, could get in my little bitty ear. The worst thing was when she started twisting back and forth to really get the dirt. No dirt in the world could have stood up to that vicious onslaught.

Grandma would walk us to church on warm summer evenings to revival meetings and Sunday night services. I can still remember the smell of peppermint weed as we walked up to church. We were always early because Grandma wanted to make sure that she got her front row seat in the choir section. She wanted everyone to see her hand pat out the time on the back of her hymn book. She always thought that she was leading the singing, and maybe she was.

Now there was a little table in the back of the church, at the corner of the pulpit, that always had a clear glass pitcher of sparkling water on it. I would have given anything that I owned for a taste of that water. It would just sit there and shine and sparkle and look so enticing, as if it were the best water in the world. I mean, it was pure agony sitting there looking at sparkling, wet, cold, refreshing water. The longer I sat there, the better it looked and the thirstier I got. My mouth would get dry and my throat would just ache as I sat looking at that water. Eventually, I could stand it no longer and I would whisper to Grandma, "I've got to have a drink of water." Finally, she would get up in front of the whole church and get us a drink of the preacher's water. And, just as we expected, it was the most delicious water in the world. Of course, by that time, stagnated water would have tasted wonderful to us two little boys.

Grandma was 46 when Mama was born so, by the time we came along and were old enough to know her, she was already up in age. I never thought of her as being anything but old and wrinkled. One day, however, I was looking at some old pictures and it dawned on me that at one time my Grandma had been young, had boyfriends, had babies and everything else that went along with youth.

One time, probably the last time that Grandma tried to cook—just to show that she hadn't lost her touch—she decided to cook an apple cobbler. Lindy, the black lady, was there helping Grandma out around the house. When Grandma opened the stove, there was a little mouse head first in the cobbler with its hind quarters sticking straight up. Well, Lindy just about fell over.

She whooped and laughed and said, "Alaw have mercy, Miss Rosey, you done cooked a rat!"

Grandma said, "Shuh, just scoop that part out." She made out like she was going to eat it, but she didn't, and neither did anyone else.

I must say right here that, although Grandma loved us, she was from the old school and thought that children shouldn't sass or talk back to their elders. She was quick on the draw with a backhand aimed for the cheek, but I think maybe her bark was worse than her bite. Sometimes when she would come at us, with her tongue clenched between her teeth and sticking out of the corner of her mouth, with hand drawn back, we thought that our heads were going to be torn clean off. Most of the time, however, we just got a little tap or a clear miss. Anyway, we learned to respect our elders or be in grave danger of a mean backhand.

When we were little, the first warm Saturdays of spring were a time for testing out the old bare feet. You know—kind of hardening them up for an all-out barefoot summer vacation. Along with bare feet and shorts came poison ivy up to the knees. And along with the poison ivy came the famous "cure" of getting washed down with Clorox bleach to dry up the itchy rash. Washing down freshly scratched poison ivy with Clorox is sort of like stepping into a nest of hornets. It sure will make you dance!

Speaking of cures, Grandma would give us a dose of kerosene, lemon juice and honey for coughs or sore throats. Now, they say that kerosene is poison. I really don't think that we were *that* sassy.

Grandma's favorite patent medicine was Camphorphenol. I think she probably thought that it would cure gangrene. For any little cut or scratch, she would say, "Just put a little Camphorphenol on it." One time, we were standing up by the garage when Grandma came backing out of the store door to lock-up for the night. She hung her heels, fell backwards and hit her head on a rock. Being the age we were, we thought it was kind of funny when her feet shot up in the air, until we saw the blood. It was a pretty bad gash. Grandma said, "Just put some Camphorphenol on it and it will be all right." And so it was.

(It must have hurt Ronnie more than Grandma, though, because he was the one who passed out when he saw the blood!)

Ronnie was an ole' tattletale. One day, I went into the back of the store and dipped an old broom into the kerosene tank. I think that I was outside before I started lighting a match to it. Anyway, Ronnie had run and told Grandma what I was up to, and when she got there, I was close enough to the door that it looked as if I had lit it up inside. Don't let anyone tell you that a Grandma past 80 can't move fast when she wants to—yelling "Scalawag! Firebug! Reform school!" I had to abandon my fiery broom to escape the fury. It was a close call, but the idea of being back-handed hard enough to be made to pee like a puppy wasn't too appealing. The fire in Grandma's eyes was about as hot as the fire on my blazing broomstick. I don't know that Grandma wasn't a little serious at the time. You would have thought that I was going to burn down the store or something. Of course, the only reason that Ronnie told on me that particular time was because he didn't have a broom of his own to light up.

Old Dr. Scott, the one who was late for my birth, made house calls to see Grandma. She thought that he was the world's greatest surgeon. When he listened to her chest and checked the pulse in her wrist, he went "Mmmm." It was a very deep sound coming from the depths of his chest and out through his nostrils. It gave her great assurance that he knew what was what and had everything under control. On several occasions, when Dr. Scott came by, we would be running out and slam-ming the door. Dr. Scott would make us go back and close the door properly. This must have stuck with me because I still don't like to slam doors. Most of the time I leave them open, just a little.

On a similar note, Daddy always had this thing about making noise when eating or smacking lips when chewing gum. Now I'm the same way. I don't like to hear myself eat.

You know, I'm sitting here in the parlor writing this page on May 9, 1993 at 3:50 in the afternoon, with the daylight coming through the windows. It's nice and comfortably cool, and I'm wondering why any-one would be nervous about passing by the door at night. I'm even sit-ting beside Madge's picture and she has her eyes right on me, yet I don't feel a bit nervous.

Madge, who was Mama's oldest sister, died when she was six years old. She would be over a hundred if she had lived. Grandma never said anything about Madge, but I guess it was a terrible, heart-breaking thing for her and Grandpop when she died. The thing about Madge's picture is that her eyes follow you wherever you go in the room. When all of us were little, we always felt kind of spooky when we went into the room by ourselves. Shucks, I think Annalee and Rosalee are still kind of spooked by it. Actually, the eyes of the picture kind of capture your attention and you don't really notice the rest of her face. To me, Madge had kind of a pretty little face, with green eyes and kind of wavy red hair that fell beside her face, over her shoulder and down her back. In the photograph, she is dressed in a white robe. Her face has a stern look but, if you stare at it closely for a while, you can almost see a smile being held back.

I also have memories of Grandma standing behind her old high-back rocking chair, dressing for bed, with the old coal oil lamp burning on the dining room table and the old mantel clock tick-tocking the time away, with a bang on the hour. Grandma always said, "Mark my words, evil communications corrupt good morals." The sign in her store window said, "Would you want to be doing what you're doing when Jesus comes?" This made a lasting impression on me.

The Madison Run Gang

Warren Dennis, whom everyone called Slick, would sometimes come to play with us. We would ask Grandma if it was okay. She would hem and haw for a while and then say, "I reckon, but you better behave." It wouldn't be hardly 10 minutes before Grandma would be hollering at Slick, "Get off my place, you scalawag, and don't come back!" Poor Slick never knew what he had done wrong and neither did we. I think maybe she never saw him mess up, either, but would run him off just in case he was messing up.

Slick was basically a good old boy and was one of the Madison Run gang when we were little. We never called ourselves a gang, though, because we were never all together at one time. Eventually, most of the gang got BB guns and, naturally being boys, this led to gun battles. The only rule was no shooting at the head.

Of course, some people didn't follow this rule. One time Ronnie and Jeep were in battle, and Jeep was behind a tree poking his head out and pulling it back. Ronnie waited until Jeep pulled his head back, then fired, and bingo—Jeep stuck his head out again just in time to stop a BB. Another time, possibly during that same battle, I was up on the top porch and Ronnie was down on the old store porch shooting it out. I looked around the corner and pop! He got me in the top of the head while I was looking down. Ronnie's Daisy Defender BB gun was unusually powerful and that BB really smarted. So, I stuck my head around the corner again and yelled, "No shooting at the head," and pop! Another BB hit me right between the eyes, dead center! I mean that really smarted, and it also ended the battle. That was getting too close to the eyes for me. On top of that, I also had a marble-sized lump on my head.

Ronnie wouldn't let anyone pick on me. He always saved me for himself. One spring, for example, I was up in the walnut tree down by the pond. I was standing on a limb minding my own business, when Ronnie climbed up so that his neck was right at my toes. It just so happened that he had a boil on the back of his neck and he said, "You better not kick my boil."

Now you try standing on a little tiny limb, holding on with both hands, with a nasty old boil one half inch away from your toes, and not move your feet. The inevitable happened. I'll give Ronnie credit, though—he didn't throw me out of the tree. He just stood on the ground and threw walnuts at me for about 15 minutes or so until he got tired. It was kind of him to finally let me down.

One time, Wiggly Mundy begged us to come over to his house to play. He had this big old dog that we were afraid of, so Wiggly tied him up while we were there. The trouble was, as soon as we finished playing and started home, Wiggly went and untied that old dog. The old dog stopped at the bridge, but we didn't know that. I don't think he really wanted the old dog to bite us; he just wanted to see us run, and run we did. At least I ran. Ronnie was riding his racing bike that Uncle Woodson had given him and he wouldn't let me on. Now I knew that if anyone was going to get bit, it was going to be me, because there was no way that I could keep up with that old racing bike and that old dog would bite the slowest man. So, with one fear-induced lunge, I grabbed the back of the seat and held on. Ronnie was always strong for his age, so when he cranked that old racing bike, I was sort of like Rick when he saw the hat at the upstairs window. My feet touched the ground every twelve or fifteen feet. Even though my brother didn't want anyone picking on me, when it came down to the nitty-gritty over getting dog bit, it was every man for himself.

As I said before, our pre-teen years were the best times we'll ever have. Mama and Daddy worked, and Grandma was old, so we pretty much had the run of the neighborhood on Saturdays and summer break. We ran the roads and the train tracks, and fished in the creek with bent straight pins for hooks. Sometimes, after hearing big blasts at the rock quarry, we would go over after quitting time and pull dynamite wire out of the crumbled rocks. And sometimes we would do a little cliff climbing.

The Lord watches out for little kids. If He didn't, we probably would have been blown up by dynamite that was still attached to the wire we collected, or been crushed by loose boulders, or fallen off the cliffs. The only person that I can remember getting hurt was William Hicks. He was halfway up a cliff when a rock came loose in one hand and mashed the thumb nail off on his other hand. He hung on, though, and didn't even cry.

One of the other things that our gang liked to do for fun was to go over behind Shirley Perkins' or Wade Browning's and swing on the vines that hung from the trees. Swinging on vines sounds pretty safe until you consider that we were 10 or 12 feet up in the air, swinging over gullies between steep hills. All of us were pretty lucky, though, because no one got a broken neck.

William Hicks, however, did get what should go in the record books as the biggest "strawberry" in history. A strawberry is when the skin is scoured off and the blood seeps out, looking kind of like the red fruit of the same name. Well, some of us were out playing Tarzan on some vines one day when William decided to show us how to make a really high and long swing. He started out good, but his Tarzan yell was cut short when the vine broke in mid-swing. When he picked himself up off the ground, half of his body looked like a strawberry. That's the last time I remember going vine swinging.

When we were little, we kind of had the run of Madison Run. Every yard, field, road and railroad track was our playground. Our favorite spot, though, was in Bob Gipson's field right on main street in "downtown" Madison Run. We played football, soccer and baseball there, and also wrestled and just had fun. It was a fairly level spot with short grass and the cow patties weren't too bad to step around. It was just an all-around good, convenient place to play.

Then one day disaster struck. A big truck loaded with lumber rolled up and started to unload right in the middle of our playing field. Carl and Thelma were building a house on the best field around. Carl and Thelma were younger then, so I'll lay the blame for this cold and callous deed on their age. It seems to me that they would have thought about their own son, Bub. Well, after 40 years, I guess it's best to let bygones be bygones.[3] We were able to move our games to a different part of the field, but it wasn't the same. The grass was coarser, the hill was steeper and the cow patties were always fresher and closer together.

We had the run of every place except Etna Estes' bass pond. She had had the pond stocked with bass after it had been dug. I know there were great fish in that pond because, on several occasions, we saw her heading back home with nice strings of bass. She was the only one, however, who fished in that pond. In the creeks, we only caught little sun perch and horned chubs. So we coveted that fish pond or, at least, the fish that were in it.

Well, needless to say, we devised a plan to get some of those fish. We collected all of the onion and feed bags that we could find, sewed them together and made a giant net that stretched across the pond. We were going to bag some big fish come nightfall. So, when darkness came, we headed out across the hill on our mission. Now, I suppose I could say that we cleaned out the pond or that Etna Estes caught us and we had to run for it. The truth, however, is that when those sacks and feed bags

---

[3] Just kidding, Carl and Thelma. —GH

got wet, they were so heavy we couldn't pull the net out. We ended up leaving it in the water. I'll bet it was full of big old bass. And I wonder what Etna thought when she saw it.

The Madison Run gang also played a variety of games. One of them was "hang on" tag. Instead of just tagging someone, you had to hang on to them and count to ten. If you could hang on to the count of ten, then the other person was "it" and had to catch someone else. Another game was "holler" hide-and-seek. This was played at night with two or three guys designated "it" and the rest free. The free ones got a count of two hundred before the "it" ones could go after them. When played fairly, the "it" ones would holler every once in a while and the free ones had to holler back. The holler would be answered by a short "yip" until the "it" ones got within a hundred feet or so of a free one. The free ones had to stay in one place until they were sighted, then they could run to avoid being tagged. It was a lot of fun running around in the dark.

Rasseling was something else. We would go to Uncle Mutt's or somewhere to watch real wrestling on TV. We watched Argentina Rocker, Gorgeous George, Lou Theas and others. We learned all kinds of holds, like "Lie the Sleeper," "Scissors," "Neck Lock," "Body Slam," "Hammer Lock," "Full Nelson," "Half Nelson," "Knee Breaker," and more. I mean that was real rasseling, not that fake stuff on TV today or that baby stuff you see in high schools. We rasseled to win, and to win meant that someone else had to say "I give up."

My favorite hold was the Knee Breaker, which involved getting my knee behind my opponent's knee and pulling his foot back towards his rear. It worked every time! Johnny was the best one to rassel. I used to think that his pain threshold was very low, but maybe he was just smart and wasn't going to let anyone put unnecessary strain on his joints. We fooled with Johnny some, like we were going to beat him up. When he was grabbed, he would holler "ow ow ow ow" real fast so that he would be turned loose. We never knew if he was really being hurt or not, so we always let go. It got so we just had to make out like we were going to grab him, and he would go "ow ow ow ow." I should point out that Johnny was a little bit smaller than the rest of us at the time.

One time, several of us were down at the spring just sitting around, busy doing nothing. Well, Johnny comes up to us with this box of laxatives that looked and smelled like chocolate. He was willing to share with the rest of us, but we declined. I heard later that Johnny ate the whole box. I also heard that it about killed him. He told his Mama that we made him eat them. Twern't so.

A tale that I heard from Poochie goes like this: Poochie and some others were out in the field one day trying to break a horse. The horse kept throwing Poochie off, so Poochie got someone to tie his feet together under the horse's belly so that he couldn't be bucked off. You can imagine what happened. Poochie slid around, upside down, under the horse, with his feet tied together above the horse's back. They said the horse just about kicked the stuffing out of Poochie before they got him untied. (I don't know for a fact that this really happened, but it was told to me as factual.)

At Halloween, we had fun doing things like turning over Uncle Sam's rabbit pen, or putting lawn chairs up on someone's roof or hedge, or blocking the road with corn shucks. Just some clean Halloween fun. Then, the next day, we would set the rabbit pen back up and get the chairs back down, while sympathizing with the owner about how dirty a trick it was for someone to have done such a thing.

One time, however, Slick heard about a now-infamous trick that was a little on the dirty rotten side. The trick was to get a paper bag, put manure in it, put it on someone's porch, then light a match to the bag and knock on the door. When the owner came to the door and saw the fire, the first thing they would do was stomp the fire out. Need I say more? I'm not saying who the trick was played on, but I will say that I didn't help, although I admit that I am guilty by association with those responsible.

On another Halloween occasion, Jeep and I came close to being murdered—very close. Peggy's boyfriend had come to see her and he was driving a fairly new '54 Ford convertible. Why in the world anyone would leave the back window unzipped on Halloween is beyond me. Not meaning to do any damage, other than having to clean gravel out of his back seat, Jeep and I proceeded to use cardboard scoops to fill his back seat up. What we didn't know was that the boyfriend had an expensive camera on the seat! Well, some of the guys who weren't a regular part of the Madison Run gang told on us.

The next thing we heard was that we had better haul freight fast because the boyfriend was coming with a bayonet in his hand, and that he was furious and meant business. To say that I was scared would be an understatement. Jeep was known for his fleetness of foot, and usually he was the fastest in the neighborhood, but that one time Jeep was eating my dust! When I looked down the road and saw that flashlight coming at a rapid pace, I found one more notch in my throttle and had those ten toes scratching gravel.

When Jeep and I split off in different directions, the boyfriend followed Jeep—I guess because he was closer. If he had followed me he would have had me because after a hundred yards or so, that burst of speed had burned out. I got half-way under a fence and couldn't go another inch, even to keep from getting stabbed.

Poor old Jeep fell in a spring and was caught. The way I heard it, he begged for his life when that bayonet was pointed at him. They said Jeep cried, "I didn't do it, you can ask my Mama!"

Now wasn't that a chicken thing to say? Of course, if I had been caught I might have pleaded worse than that. When you are 10 or 11 years old, and a bayonet is pointed at your throat, you will say a lot of things. The boyfriend must have figured that he had taught us a lesson because he let Jeep go and didn't come after me. All he had to do was follow the thumping of my heart and I would have been easy to find.

We used to hear about boys swiping watermelons from gardens, but no one around Madison Run grew any. So, one night us guys stole a couple of onions from a garden. I have to say, they were kind of tasty, mostly because of the adventurous way in which they were acquired.

Another time, Uncle Albert had some of those picturesque corn shucks sitting around in a field, like the ones you see in those scenic calendar photographs. They were standing in a way that made it possible for a person to run, dive through the air and land on the shucks without getting hurt. We had fun, but we over did it. Uncle Albert was a little upset and started looking for the culprits. Ronnie, Bub and Wiggly ended up shucking all of the flattened corn because they were the only ones who admitted to the deed. I think Uncle Albert came out to the good on that one.

Brothers on the Loose

When my brother Ronnie and I were a couple of years younger, we liked to play Superman and Batman. We dressed for the part by donning a pair of long johns, with a pair of jockey shorts over these, and a feed sack for a cape. That cape really set that suit off! Wearing this get-up, we would head for the railroad bank in front of Carl and Thelma McClendon's house. We would get a running start and go sailing over the bank with our capes flowing in the wind behind us, landing deftly on our feet beside the railroad tracks. I think that our capes gave us more lift and helped us to fly farther. At least it seemed as if they did. I mean that was flying!

Pigeon hunting was another thing we did to have fun. It took at least two people. One person would shine the flashlight in the birds' eyes to blind them. The other would climb up in the top of the barn to grab a pigeon and climb back down. All of this was done in pitch darkness. The only other light was the reflection from the pigeons' eyes. The guys

in all of those new adventure movies don't have anything on us. We did-
n't have "stand-ins" for the dangerous parts!

I used to hate working in the garden. Daddy would say in his most I-
mean-business voice, "Now you boys get out early before the sun gets
too hot and pull those weeds and hoe those rows of beans or whatever
they need." I don't care how early it was—that old sun would be there to
turn on the heat. I was miserable. The ground was hard. The weeds
hated to be pulled and grew extra-long roots deliberately. Oh, how that
sun would bear down. Sweat in the eyes, itching body, sore knees, sore
hands—my Mama and Daddy and Grandma must hate me.

Ronnie would always finish his row first and wouldn't help me do
mine. It was at that moment that I hated summer vacation and wished
that school would start. Then, that last weed at the end of the row
would fall by the wayside, and boy-oh-boy, it would suddenly be a great
day to go fishing, climb a few trees, swim in the creek or just lie around
in the shade doing nothing.

We had a favorite apple tree that we played in all the time. It was a
giant of an apple tree, with a huge trunk and limbs that stretched way
out and way up. The limbs were slick and smooth from all of our climbing, and we had a funny-shaped piece of metal that fit perfectly in the
crotch of our tree. It made a great tree house, and four or five of us boys
would sit on it and talk, plotting our next adventure. Now it's almost
too small for just me to sit on. That piece of metal must have shrunk
over the years!

The old tree blew over in a storm years ago, but our metal "tree
house" is still at the old home place.

Glass bottles were made to be broken by little boys. No boy worth his
salt took the job lightly in my neighborhood. There were few, if any,
bottles laying around in one piece. I have to say that Ronnie, with his
deadly right arm, took the job almost to fanaticism. In fact, if it had

been up to us, future archaeologists would have had a hard time finding an intact glass artifact. We were very serious about the job.

Uncle Nat (Mead Mundy) kept two old work horses in our orchard when we were little. He used them for plowing and discing the fields around the neighborhood. He got his plowing done with a lot of gee-hawing, by jingoes, cat manure and old boots, and a lot of other colorful language.

The two horses, Dan and Slim, got so they would put their heads through our swing ropes so that we would feed them apples and such. We would also climb up in the tree and get down on their backs while they stood there. One time we got the bright idea to tie bells on the horses' halters. Every time the horses would walk, the bells would jingle and frighten the horses into running. This made the bells jingle louder, so the horses would run even faster. Uncle Nat didn't appreciate that very much because the old horses really worked up a lather trying to get away from those bells. In fact, he got mad as a hornet and even told Grandma on us. As well as I can remember, he took old Dan and Slim away shortly after that.

One time when we were little, Uncle Woodson gave Ronnie an old Army pup tent. Well, we begged, pleaded and pestered Mama to please let us camp out.

Mama said, "Now ya'll know you won't stay out there all night."

We replied, "Oh, yeah, Mama, we'll stay out. We won't be scared. Just you watch."

So she said, "All right then."

We got that old tent set up, had our blankets all laid out and were just comfy cozy. Just as safe and snug as a bug in a rug. That is, until Mama turned out the last light in the house. We were attacked immediately by unseen ghosts, snakes, bears, mummies and whatever else terrifies little kids when the lights go out. All of those monsters must have really had it in for us that night. Heck, those athletes that do that wall climb didn't have anything on us. We scaled the bottom porch, shinnied up the post to the top porch, and went over the rail, with all of those mummies, ghosts, bears and snakes snapping and clawing at our heels. We barely escaped.

All of this took less than 10 seconds and who knows how many years off of our lives. By the time Mama went upstairs that evening, we were already in bed, covered up. Of course, if Mama had known just how close we had come to being torn limb from limb or eaten alive, she wouldn't have thought it was so funny!

There used to be some old chicken houses around the home place that made pretty good playhouses. One in particular was way up at the end of the property all by itself. We had it all cleaned up real neat, nice and cozy. One day we were in there with the sun streaming through the door and the window, when it dawned on us that this would be a great place to spend the night. So, with our usual begging and pleading, Mama finally gave in and said all right. She probably figured that we wouldn't last long out there, anyway.

So, along about night fall, we got our stuff together and, with an old oil lamp, made the journey to our chicken house and set up housekeeping for the night. The darker it got, the darker and longer the shadows got from the light that that old oil lamp cast. I had already started to think that maybe this wasn't too good an idea, staying out in a gloomy, dreary, shadowy, spooky chicken house. Then, an old spider came crawling out of a crack in the floor, spreading its legs out so that it looked the size of a silver dollar. We came to the quick conclusion that this was not a good place to be after dark. Boy-oh-boy, a spider that big could kill half of Madison Run. If a spider that big could get through a crack, what would stop snakes, rats or just about anything else that wanted to get in? Needless to say, it didn't take near as long to get to the house in the dark as it did to get to the chicken coop at dusk. I don't remember playing in that old chicken house again after that. I guess that feeling of fear kind of ruined it for us. Wherever you are when shadows lengthen and darkness falls, things and places just don't look the same or as safe anymore, especially to little boys.

We were up to Baltimore one time, visiting Bill and Rosalee. Bill told us some tall tales about this old Japanese sword that he had gotten in WWII. The sword had red grease on it (I guess to keep it from rusting), but Bill had us thoroughly convinced that it was Jap blood. He also told us that he had gotten shot in the arm. Later, I learned that Bill had shot at an Army tank just to see if it was really bullet-proof, and the bullet ricocheted and hit him. He got a Purple Heart for being wounded in action.

Well, anyway, later on, we were going down the cellar steps. Just as we got to the bottom, Ronnie said, "Look, over there is a Jap!"

It was dark outside and the basement light made a reflection in the glass that looked like someone looking in. Bill already had us wide-eyed and it didn't take much more for our imaginations to take off. Also, since Ronnie was older and saw it first, it didn't take much to convince me that it was a Jap. It was a good thing that basement door wasn't closed, because we were moving so fast coming up that it would have been torn off its hinges! Bill still thinks it was funny.

Speaking of Bill, he's a person that kids take a liking to. One time, he said that he would give me a quarter if I could put a pea through an inch-wide hole with a soda straw. I won and he paid.

When we were little, Aunt Lelia and Uncle Willie Bowers would come for a visit at Grandma's store. Aunt Lelia was Grandma's sister. We would ask, "Grandma, can we give Uncle Willie a cake out of the store?" She always agreed and he would always give us a quarter, which was generous, because at that time a cake only cost a nickel. Grandma had to sell a dozen cakes to make that much profit. When Aunt Lelia and Uncle Willie came for Christmas dinner, it was a grand time. After dinner, we would sit in the parlor and listen to Uncle Willie tell tales about times long ago. He would laugh and slap his knee and get all excited about the story that he was telling. It's hard to describe just how enjoyable a time that was.

I remember a Mr. Seargent who used to come by Grandma's store. He sold Watkins products and some of the best, if not the best, vanilla pudding pie filling in the world. Sometimes, if we begged and pleaded and looked real pitiful, Mama would buy us some. That pie filling was the only thing that we liked about Mr. Seargent because every time he came by, he would grab at us and say he was going to take us with him. That scared us to death and we would run like crazy. It was kind of a let down when we got older and realized that he didn't really want to catch us.

Then there was old Charlie, who would occasionally come by and sit at Grandma's store. He had a growth on the inside of his mouth and sometimes, if we asked him, he would stick it out of the side of his mouth and let us look at it. We were fascinated by that thing. 'Course, it didn't take much to entertain us, anyhow.

When we were little, radio was our entertainment because televisions were kind of scarce. In fact, I was probably 10 or 11 before I even saw one. Daddy told us there was something like a radio that you could see a picture in, along with the sound. So Ronnie and I peered through the cracks of the speaker in our radio to see if there was a picture inside.

One program on the radio was a scary one. I think it was the Inner Sanctum, but we called it the Creaking Door because it always started off with the sound of the door of a tomb creaking open. One story that I remember was about a man who was buried alive. The people who buried him were sitting in their house when the windows shattered out. The man who was buried was calling for help from the grave in a real ghostly, scary-sounding voice. There was another story in which a mummy had come to life and was going around getting people. His feet would go "thump, thump, thump" and someone would scream. I tell you one thing, it would make the hair stand up on your head. It was scary going to bed and cutting the lights off after hearing all of that. In a lot of ways, radio was better than TV because you had to use your imagination to get a picture, and some of the pictures in our minds could be awfully vivid. I could almost see that man in the grave fighting and clawing to get out, and that old mummy stumping along with arms raised, ready to grab his victim.

Other shows included Bobby Benson and the B-Bar-B Ranch, Sky King and his plane called the Song Bird, an Indian called Golden Arrow, Dragnet and the Lone Ranger, just to name a few. These shows starred people who seemed bigger than life on the radio. When some of them came out on TV, it kind of brought them down. To us little boys, they just weren't as heroic-looking as they had sounded on the radio.

One time, we had a little part beagle, part basset hound, with the biggest feet you ever saw. One of us (it had to have been Ronnie) got the bright idea to get the little dog drunk. We went down the shoulders of the road and picked up all of the whiskey bottles we could find that still had a little whiskey left in them, and we poured them down the dog's throat. Then we got the sherry wine that Dr. Scott had prescribed to Grandma for her heart. We poured it on bread and the little dog ate it as fast as we gave it to him.

After a few minutes, that dog was plastered. He started to stagger around and we were afraid that Mama would find out, so we took him down to the spring and put him over in the briar patch. By this time, the little dog was really feeling good and he was singing at the top of his lungs, "Aaaooooooooww, aaaooooooooooww."

About that time, Preacher Leseuer came by for a visit and the dog was still down in the briar patch just carrying on. Mama asked, "What's wrong with that dog?" Of course we said that we didn't know, but I guess we must have acted suspicious, because Mama said, "Ya'll go get that dog." We set the dog down in front of Mama and the preacher, and he went staggering and flopping around the yard. (The dog, not the preacher.) I don't think Preacher Leseuer knew what was wrong, but Mama did. At least she saw the humor in the situation and just told us not to do it any-more. I bet that dog had a hangover supreme the next morning.

One of my chores was drawing water from the well. The well house had a pulley with a chain on it and a bucket on each end, so that when you pulled one bucket up, the other bucket went down to refill. Mama would always keep an eye on us when we were around the well. She would warn, "You be careful around that well." I never could figure out why they made me draw the water if the well was so dangerous. So one day I got this great idea for a prank. When Mama went back into the house to do something, I pulled a bucket of water half-way up to the top and then let go of the chain. The bucket of water fell back down into the well with a rattle of chain and a splash of the bucket when it hit the water. Then the other bucket hit the pulley at the top of the well house with a spectacular sounding crash. While this was going on, I ran around behind the well and hid.

Mama came flying out of the door screaming, thinking that I was down in the well. When Mama screamed, I knew instantly that my little prank had backfired. I came flying around the well hollering "Here I am, Mama! Here I am." When she saw me, she just broke down and boo-hoo'ed and cried. I felt so bad that I never tried anything like that again.

Seasons

In winter, Zion Baptist Church was heated by two great, big, cast iron wood stoves and everyone sat up close to the heat. Sometimes Uncle Albert would have his little chew of tobacco and discreetly spit into the stove door. During Christmas plays there was always a nativity scene and boys young and old participated.

On hot summer Sunday nights or revival nights, I remember trying to get a seat by the open, screen-less windows to catch a little breeze coming by. The moths flew in and out around the lights while we listened to the old hell-fire and brimstone sermons. Ronnie and I would stand and sing with the grown-ups. We would sing at the top of our lungs, "ee awww, eee awww, eee awww," because to us that's what the singing sounded like and we just wanted to take part.

Everyone should have such memories. In the wintertime, we lived for the first snowfall, so that we could get off from school and go sleigh riding.[4] We sometimes got so excited at the prediction of snow that we would get the wood in without being told to do it. Our bedroom was upstairs in the room farthest from the heat so, other than being out of the wind, it seemed just as cold as outside. I remember putting flatirons

---

4 During my generation, as well as Gary's, the term "sleigh riding" referred to riding a sled down a hill. It did not mean being drawn by a horse in a sleigh. It wasn't until I had grown up and met people from other regions of the country that I learned such activity could also be called "sledding" or even "tobogganing," (although I still assert that tobogganing can only be performed on actual toboggans and not on other types of sleds). —Ed.

in bed, wrapped in towels to keep them from burning our feet. We sat them on the stove to get them hot first. The first couple of minutes in a bed that is as cold as the outdoors is a real awakening experience. In the mornings, it was especially bitter getting out of that warm bed into the freezing cold air. It didn't take us long to run down the stairs to where Mama, Daddy or Grandma would have a hot fire burning. We would back up close to the stove until it got painfully hot, then turn around to bake the other side.

One time I had a problem getting warm after I had gone to bed. I folded blankets together until they were a foot thick but I was still cold. Then I discovered that in the straw tick that I was sleeping on, the feathers had moved to one side and the only things under me were two thin pieces of cloth. A good fluffing cured that problem.

In the summer, we used to sleep up on the top porch. Sometimes it would rain and the mist would blow in on our faces. We would hunker down in the covers and it was the coziest feeling in the world. At other times, honey bees would come out of their nests at night and try to get at us, and we would pull a sheet over our heads until they went away.

Trains would come flying by with the wheels streaming fire way back from what was called a hot box. (The grease packing on the wheels would get hot and catch on fire.) Sometimes the trains would stop at night to switch cars to sidetrack. This always seemed spooky, especially after two men had been killed along the tracks. The cars would just sit there and make these quiet little hissing noises while waiting to be unhooked. You could almost imagine ghosts walking along the tracks. Then, we would hear a big bang as the engine started, then bang, bang, bang as each car started off. It would be a relief for us, I guess because we figured that any ghosts in the area left with the train. Of course, we only got spooked on dark, moonless nights.

One thing about sleeping on the porch was that going to the bathroom was pretty convenient. We just went over the railing, which was a whole lot better than using the thunder jug.

When we were little, we slept in the same room with Grandma. Sometimes when we talked too long, Grandma would peck on the bed rail with her fingernail. She would go peck, peck, peck, and we'd get real quiet and ask, "Grandma, is that you?" Then we'd hear that peck, peck, peck again, but Grandma would say nothing. We always thought that it was her, but we were never too sure; after all, that old parlor door wasn't all that far away. Our only option was to lie still and quiet until sleep overtook us.

Other memories include lying on our backs and spitting water into the air to feel the coolness of it falling back; being out in the orchard eating a variety of apples all summer; waking up on summer mornings with the birds singing outside of our bedroom windows or just off the porch; everything looking so fresh and new; and the joy of a new day starting. Ah, those sweet times, when we were under twelve, that seemed as if they would never end.

Daddy would take us to town with him on Saturdays and give us each a quarter. With some careful shopping, we could buy a comic book, a drink, some candy and a toy at one of the three five-and-dime stores in town. Sometimes we would even get an extra quarter or two, depending on Daddy's finances or charitableness. On those three quarter days, we really felt the power of a dollar.

We had this old oil stove sitting in the dining room. I think Daddy first had it down at his barber shop. Anyway, it was about 16 inches in diameter and about 4 ½ feet tall. The thing really put out a lot of heat, and the only thing between us and the fire was a thin sheet of metal. Every once in a while, someone would turn on the oil and forget to light it, or the match would go out, resulting in a lot of oil running into that old stove. The next time that it was lit, the fire would go out of control. I mean, that thing would jump and roar, and turn cherry red from top to bottom—even up the chimney pipe to where it went into the wall.

Ronnie came by just as I was writing this, so I asked him if he remembered that old oil stove. He said, "Yeah, it would go 'whump,

whump, whump, woof, woof, woof, whoooo.' And it went 'sssss' when it burned your arm!"

Unusual Characters

Mr. Hall, who goes by the alias "Papa," told me a story the other day about Mutt Hicks. He was Uncle Mutt to us kids. Seems like when hurricane Hazel came through in '52 or '55, Uncle Mutt was running the old store down by the tracks—the one on the piney woods side of the tracks.[5] It just so happened that a man who worked on the pipeline, called a pipeliner, was there. Since the pipeliner was from the coast of Texas, he was used to seeing the types of clouds that meant a bad storm was brewing. Well, he told Uncle Mutt that he had better get out of that rickety old building before the storm arrived.

Uncle Mutt said, "Naw, man, I ain't scared of no storm."

It wasn't too long after that that the wind came up and pieces started to separate from that old building. That was bad enough, but when the wind became so strong that it blew a couple of old hound dogs off of the front porch, Uncle Mutt came to the conclusion that it was time to vacate the premises. The closest cover was a railroad culvert in front of the store. That was all right until it started to rain so hard that it flooded the culvert. Uncle Mutt ended up back underneath the old store to weather out the storm after all. I think that storm was the same one that tore the big porch off of Mr. Hall's house. It was also during this storm that Bub rolled off the bed while sucking his bottle and broke his neck. He's lucky he wasn't paralyzed.

---

5 Bubba Lutz claims that Hazel hit in 1955, but I think he just wanted to argue. —GH

(According to the 1998 World Almanac and Book of Facts, Hurricane Hazel hit Haiti, the eastern United States and eastern Canada in October, 1954, and killed 347 people. —Ed.)

Archie Branham, or "Oychie," as his wife Goldie called him, was Daddy's buddy. I guess they were kind of compatible since both of them were crippled. Archie got his good foot caught in a hay bailer and it was cut off. He lost the whole leg up to his hip because of infection. Anyway, Archie would come down to our house, and he and Daddy would work on little projects together, like working in the garden or in the shop. Archie died a right good while before Daddy. I know Daddy missed him. Goldie used to come down and stay with Grandma while Mama was at work. She sure didn't do it for the money, because Mama couldn't pay much. Goldie was a good-hearted lady and she was good to Grandma. Goldie requested that Ronnie, Peter, James and I be pallbearers at her funeral. I don't remember who the other pallbearers were, but I've always considered it an honor to be asked to be one of the pallbearers for someone's funeral.

One time, Aunt Fanny Mae was down for a visit. Mama was going to town to get something, so she asked Aunt Fannie Mae to go along. Well, Aunt Fannie Mae had her nightgown on and was ready for bed.

Mama said, "Aw, come on, it's dark. No one is going to see you."

So, with a lot of giggling and laughing and speculation about what would happen if the car broke down, off we went. It's a good thing that I went along because the car started to miss and jump about two or three miles down the road, and then it died. Aunt Fannie Mae thought that Mama was kidding her at first, but there we sat, out of gas, with Aunt Fannie sitting there in her nightgown on Route 15! I don't know what they would have done if I hadn't been along to run back and get Uncle Sam to bring some gas. I guess it would have looked kind of funny to see an old lady walking down the highway at night with her nightgown flapping in the breeze.

Grandpop was a little mischievous. He used to have long counters down each side of the store and people had the habit of jumping up to sit on them. Grandpop had a remedy for this. He drilled little holes in the counter and, when someone sat over a hole, he would pull a string at the end of the counter where he sat. This caused a needle to pop-up through each hole just enough to stick each offender in the butt and scare them into jumping off the counter. Grandpop caught one young lady sitting on the counter and he stabbed her in the rump with a needle. He got a good reaction—a lot of cussing and yelling. She didn't think it was funny, but Grandpop did. Another time, when he was building a new johnny house, I mean a brand new two-holer, he called Grandma out like it was really something important. Then he got her to sit on the board, took a pencil and marked around her bottom to get what he called a perfect fit.

The first time I saw Grandpop, that I can remember, he had cut down an old cedar tree in the front yard. He and Ronnie were skinning the bark off to make it a light pole. Grandpop had a great big draw knife and Ronnie had a little tiny one. They were a working team. It looked like fun, but I guess they thought that I was too little to try it. I guess three or four was kind of young to handle a knife. Anyway, I tried it some years later and it wasn't that much fun. That old pole, by the way, stood for many years, until Uncle Woodson took it down.

Garland and Earl Coates were a little younger than the rest of us. Sometimes, when some of us would be hanging around the railroad crossing, their mama, Marylee, would send them to Harlow's store for something. They had to come right by us older boys. None of us ever bothered them, but Earl always had that look, like maybe he didn't trust us and was suspicious about what we might do. They would come hurrying by, looking straight ahead, but you could tell that Earl was watching us out of the corner of his eye. They looked right cute, about the same size, shoulder to shoulder, real close, with Garland on the protective side of Earl. Once in while, someone would cuss at them a little bit just to hear Earl cuss back and say, "You're the same," while still looking straight ahead. I believe that if anyone had made an offensive move on Earl, they would have had a tough little customer on their hands. He had the look and talk that made you not want to try anything. I guess, also, that we didn't do anything because all of us still needed each other to play with at other times.

I remember Mr. Roberts sitting on his front porch, in the sun, with his hands painfully twisted with arthritis. His old bull dog, Turk, was always in the yard standing guard. The only way to get in to see Mr. Roberts was to throw Turk a stick and run for the porch while he chased it.

Water

I was just sitting here thinking about the things we did to have fun when we were kids. Probably the times that we spent just lazing around playing in water were the most enjoyable.

It seems to me that the best thing a kid could have would be a loving, Christian home, with a warm bed and plenty to eat. The next best thing to have would be a little stream of water trickling out of a spring or flowing down a creek nearby. There is nothing like a little water to play in to keep kids' minds occupied and out of trouble for hours on end.

Having a pool of water to play in sure made for some contented and happy times, especially if the water was running down a ditch or a nice little creek. Of course, in a pinch, after a big old thunder shower rolled by, there would be little temporary streams flowing and they did nicely while they lasted. We would get some rocks, scrap wood or anything else to dam up water, and we would create a big old pond in a roadside ditch, at least for a while. Shucks, we could have put the Army Corps of Engineers to shame with our dam building, at least in our minds.

One place that we played on occasion was over in Uncle Albert's field in front of our house, about 150 yards after crossing the tracks. There was a little ditch that was really a run-off from a wet weather spring, and it always had at least a little water in it. I don't remember it ever going completely dry when we were little.

The best creek, though, was a creek fed by springs coming off of the Stricklers' place. It ran in front of Uncle Albert's place, about 300 feet down the hill from his house. This was the same creek in which we occasionally fished, using bent straight pins tied on to the end of a piece of string to catch horned chubbs or sometimes a small sun perch.

Then there was a spring over behind Jeep Perkins' house that had a pretty good stream flowing from it. The Gipson's also had a good spring that the water ran out of and ended up in the same ditch as the Perkins' stream. Those streams ran under the road through a culvert that Slick, at one time, had us thoroughly convinced was the entrance to an old iron mine. Eventually, all of that water ended up in Madison Run creek.

Madison Run creek ran down the edge of Uncle Sam's hog pen and through Harlow's pasture field. That is the field in which we did most of our major swimming and damming up after we got a little older. It also picked up the water coming out of a real nice, deep spring on the Harlow's place. That was the same spring that someone once stole our drinks out of after we had to abandon our camp site in the midst of a terrible thunder storm that surprised us in the middle of the night.

There were a couple of other springs on the Harlow place, but we never messed around in them because they were too swampy and snakey-looking. Come to think of it, us kids used Uncle Raymond and Aunt Wilmeta's place so often to camp, swim, sleigh ride, play hide-and-seek and just hang out, that we probably could have applied for squatters' rights.

Back up in front of the Gipson place, about 400 feet down from the front of the house, was a spring underneath a great big maple tree. It had a little water in it but it wasn't much fun to play in because it was too muddy. I think the tree roots probably slowed the water down or something. That was the same spring, by the way, that Jeep fell in when he was trying to get away from Peggy's irate boyfriend. [6]

---

[6] Gary's fond memories of playing in water suggest that his was a transitional generation in the United States, when the locations of springs and streams went from being a matter of survival for rural farmers to a matter of fun for children. Today, I suspect that the tremendous growth in urban and suburban development has made the location of springs and streams a moot issue for the average American, including children. It might seem trivial, but it helps to demonstrate just how different America is in the early 21st century than it was in the early 20th century. —Ed.

THE
TEEN YEARS

When I was 13, Uncle Sam got me my first job working for a man filling candy and cigarette vending machines. Filling the machines was easy, but sitting in the little storage room, putting pennies under the cellophane of cigarette packs (to give back change for a quarter), was boring.[7] Anyway, sitting at a little machine all day long on a Saturday, sticking a little blue blade under the cellophane of each pack, stomping a pedal with my foot to insert four pennies into the pack, then looking across the room at all of those cases of cartons stacked to the ceiling, and thinking of those thousands of packs to go, really made for a long, boring day.

When I wasn't putting pennies under cellophane, I was on the road with John Bradshaw filling vending machines. It was a nice break from sitting in that little room punching pennies all day. Until we ended up in Culpeper, that is, where John would always stop at this little restaurant on the edge of town. He would order a chitterling. Or is it a chitlin sandwich?[8] He offered to get me something, but I wouldn't eat anything that came out of that place. Just to think about eating guts was bad

---

[7] The cigarette machines at the time would not return change and smokes usually cost around 21 cents a pack. —*GH*

[8] The terms "chitterling" and "chitlins" are synonymous. Both refer to the intestines of hogs, especially when prepared as food. —*Ed.*

enough, but to sit there watching him eat those things, and smelling them…ugh! Listening to those little slurpy, smacking sounds, and seeing those guts hanging from between those two slices of bread, was a real stomach-turner. I couldn't help watching, though, even if it was revolting.

Hot Rod Hogsten

We had a good buddy when we were teens whose name was Ernie. His full name was Ernst Amiel Barwich. His father was a German soldier who had fought against the Allies in World War II and had ended up a Russian prisoner of war. He had been an unwilling foe of the Allies, however, and brought his family to the United States after the war.

We first met Ernie when he came riding over one day on his little motor bike, trying to find out who in the neighborhood was flying model airplanes. From then on we were good friends, from about the age of 13 until Ernie was killed in a car wreck at the age of 23 in August 1963. I guess Ernie was the first and most heart-breaking loss that we had had up to that point.

(When Jackie and I got married in 1961, we didn't have money to buy much of anything, much less a television. So here comes Ernie one day with a brand spanking new 19-inch Motorola TV, complete with antenna pole and wire. He even installed the antenna, all for a wedding present. Then for our anniversary he gave us a nice brass door knocker, which we still have. Ernie ate supper with us one evening and the way he carried on you would have thought that he was eating food fit for a king. What greater compliment could he have given my new bride than to let her know she was a good cook?)

I really had not been that anxious to get my driver's license when I turned 15 because Ronnie and Ernie both had theirs, so it wasn't like I was stranded or anything. Eventually, though, certain circumstances got me interested in getting my license. Ronnie, Wiggly and I started triple dating together, with Ronnie and his date riding in the front seat and Wiggly and I in the back with our dates. It was real cozy and close, which made it a whole lot easier to steal one of those earth-shattering kisses from those wonderfully soft, sweet lips. Whew! I think I'm getting a little mushy and corny here, but when Ronnie got tired of dating that other girl, my mode of transportation came to an end. That's when I got my driver's license, so I wouldn't miss any of those kisses. Shucks, I would have walked 10 miles for one of those sweet kisses.

Actually, I did walk five miles in a blizzard one night just so I could stand outside in a freezing phone booth for two hours, talking to the sweetest girl that ever was. And I didn't even feel a chill. I had met her one night when we were over at Rollins' Grill getting a hamburger. These two girls came in to buy a pack of gum or something. They only lived about 500 feet down the street, so we offered them a ride home. They accepted, albeit with some concern that their mamas would find out. As they were getting out of the car, I just happened to have this little piece of mistletoe in my hand, so I held it over the head of one of the girls. Since it was Christmas, I gave her a big kiss on the lips and wham! zing! bam! zowee! I was caught hook, line and sinker, and I've remained that way for more than 40 years. That was a kiss to remember.

Anyway, we all got to be hot rodders in one way or another after we got our driver's licenses. Ernie had a big hand in guiding us in the fine art of spinning wheels, speed shifting and drag racing. Mama would have fainted if she had ever known what her automobiles were going through. Sometimes when I wanted to hear some tires squeal and see some smoke fly, I would put that old '51 Ford into reverse, back up about 30 miles per hour, shift up into second and then down into first gear, and pop the clutch out. While still going backwards at 30 mph, the tires would be spinning forward at 100 mph. With the engine screaming wide open and the air cleaner off to give it more power, the carburetor sucking air would give out a sound that is hard to describe. Along with the fearsome squall of tire rubber wrenching itself loose from hard pavement, rubber smoke would billow up all around the car. It made a sight and sound that was hard to believe. And to 15 and 16 year old boys, I must say the sight and sound was most lovely. One day I measured the black marks that were left and they measured out to 214 feet!

We had a number of special hot rodding terms, such as "squeal a wheel," "burn some rubber," "peal out," "get a wheel," "get down on it," "turn it on," "dust him out," "dig out," and "floor board it," just to name a few.

One time, Hot Rod Seal (his real name was Aubrey) was down in front of the "Green Door" in his 1947 Ford coupe, bragging to us about how he could spin his tires and speed shift into second gear without moving.[9] Hot Rod proceeded to wind that little 80 horsepower, flat head V8 up until it was screaming like it was in agony. Of course, the air cleaner was off to give it more power and that added to the noise. It went something like Whoonnnnneeeahhhhhnn. That's as close as I can get to spelling out the sound and it's still not doing it justice. Those little flat head Fords had a sound all their own.

Anyway, at the peak of that whoonnnnneeeahhhhhnn, Hot Rod dropped the clutch and there was a tremendous bang underneath the little Ford. The engine screamed even louder since there weren't enough teeth left intact in the transmission or differential to slow it down. Needless to say, poor old Hot Rod had to do a little hoofing for several weeks till he could scrape together enough money to buy replacement parts. Hot Rod had flat out missed a gear. Well, he might not have missed it, but he kind of hit two at the same time, and that doesn't work.

---

[9] The "Green Door" was an old store building near Gary's parents' house that had, not surprisingly, a green door. The building no longer exists but, at the time, Gary and his friends would occasionally hang out there. —*Ed.*

Ol' Hot Rod also turned his old A model over on the sharp curve by our house, the same curve that Etna Estes and Thornton Fry had a head-on collision on a few years earlier. In addition, Hamilton Knight turned his '40 Ford over on the curve down at Harlow's store. There were two different versions of why it happened. One was that he was just trying to see how fast he could take the curve; the other was that he and Tootie had had a little lover's spat, and Hamilton had gotten a little reckless. And that was before they were married. However it was, the little green '40 Ford was a total loss.

Earl Watson was a right smart hot rodder, too. He had a little black '47 Ford coupe that, as we used to say, would flat out walk the dog. In layman's terms, that means go fast. I was in love with that car. In fact, I bought one to fix up, but never quite got around to doing it. It wouldn't have been the same as Earl's, anyway.

One night, after dropping Jackie off after our Saturday night date, I was headed home when this automobile came up behind me. It was close enough to see that it was Earl's shiny, black '47 Ford. That called for floor boarding it to see if I could dust him out. After a time, I could tell that there wasn't any space opening up between me and Earl's car. In fact, the distance seemed to be tightening up a little bit at a time. He got so close that I couldn't even see his headlights. Then there came this gentle bumper to bumper tap from the front of Earl's '47 to the back end of Mama's '51 Ford that I was driving.

I mean the pedal was to the metal, the foot was in the floor. I was stretched out, and turning it on, and the '51 Ford was screaming wide open. As well as I can remember, even clipping along at about 95 miles per hour, Earl was still pushing me from behind. I don't even think it would have helped much to have had the air cleaner off and a new set of plugs installed—that little '47 would flat out get it.

Another time, Ernie and I were messing around in Ernie's '47 Ford coupe. His was dark green. Some way or other, we ended up in a race with Harvey Powell, with Earl driving Ernie's '47 Ford. Harvey had a '51

Plymouth all fixed up and looking nice, but looks just won't do anything to help a 6-cylinder Plymouth run with a flat head '47 Ford. To make it fair, Harvey had about a 10 car-length head start.

So down the road we went, past the Woodberry Forest road and over the next hill, which was where Earl whipped out to pass Harvey. Harvey proceeded to be a poor sport. When Earl started to pass him, Harvey cut over into our lane to cut us off. Earl had to drive all of the way off of the pavement to keep from having a humongous wreck. Due to Earl's expert driving, we avoided an accident and won the race, too.

The Accident

When we were young, Jane Lutz and I were involved in a car accident together. The way I figure, it must have happened back in the 1950s. The way it happened was, I had snuck Mama's '51 Ford over to town on the pretense of going to Harlow's store to pick up some little item. But all the while my intention was to go over to town and pick Jackie up from her after school job at Rollins' meat market and give her a ride home. After all, she would have had to walk if I didn't, and that would have been all of 600 feet. And that's a long way to walk with all of the wolves around at the time.

Upon arriving at town, in the first car that I met was my girl riding down the street with someone else. I practically had stolen my Mama's car to give her a ride home, and there was that sorry hound dog trying to move in on me.

When leaving home, I hadn't noticed that the gas hand was in a dangerously low position, or maybe I did and figured it was worth the chance just so I could see my girl for a few minutes. Anyway, as I was headed back home—and if I had had a tail it would have been dragging—along about where Mama had run out of gas with Aunt Fanny Mae riding in her night gown, I ran out of gas. I was trying to coast the car as far as it would go to save some walking and it had slowed considerably. I was keeping my eyes on the rear view mirror so that if a car came up from behind I could pull over to let it by.

Just as I was getting ready to cross a little bridge, I looked in the mirror and saw a car coming up behind at what looked to me like a fast rate of speed, and there was no place for me to pull over. While still pretty far back, the driver of the other car saw me and hit the brakes. Since it was raining and the road was slick, the other car started to slide sideways. I could do nothing but coast along, scrunch my shoulders up, grit my teeth and wait. When I saw that big old '54 Pontiac coming down the road sideways, it crossed my mind that there was a good chance there was going to be a right good sized wreck in just a second or two. Then wham, wham, and Mama's old '51 took a giant leap forward.

After stopping the Ford and jumping out, I looked back and there were two wrecked cars behind me. The blue Pontiac was over the creek bank and there was a brown '56 Chevrolet sitting in the road, steam spewing from its crushed radiator. And there was Jane, crawling around on hands and knees on the shoulder of the road.

I think Jane was thrown out of the car as it went over the bank, and it was a miracle that she wasn't injured seriously. I think, but don't remember for sure, that Jane might have had a neck strain or something. The lady in the other car wasn't injured, though her automobile sustained the most damage. Both of the other cars were total losses, but Mama's old Ford only had a couple of hundred dollars' worth of damage done to it.

The lady who was driving the '56 Chevrolet was charged with the accident and got a ticket. It seemed like she hit Jane and knocked her into me; at least, that's the way I think it happened. Also, she was driving while intoxicated. I don't know if the trooper charged her with DUI but, when I left the scene, he still had her sitting in the police car.

Jane probably knows more about what happened than me because she was the one that got squashed in the middle. I'll have to ask her about it some time.

I think that if I hadn't been going so slow, and if Jane and the other lady had been going a little slower, and if the other lady hadn't been drinking, and if it hadn't been raining, and if I had pulled over sooner, and if we all had not been on the road at the same time, and if it had been another day, then the whole incident might not have happened. Come to think of it, Jackie was the whole cause of the incident. I wouldn't even have been on the road had it not been for her.

Later, I asked Jane if there was any difference in the way that she remembered the accident than the way I did. She said that I had it all about right, except for the fact that on the one day that she happened to have holes in her underwear, that would be the day she would end up being involved in an accident and going to the hospital.

THE
ADULT YEARS

When we were young, we never thought that the days of sunny blue skies, eating apples in the tree house, swimming in the creek, walking the rails, sliding down snowy hills, playing cowboys and Indians, and having Grandmas would ever end. Thoughts like that didn't intrude into our happy, blissful world.

It has been said, though, that you can never go home again. I take this to mean that the old faces, loved ones, old friends and places, won't ever come back or be the same again. That has a ring of finality to it, but I'm looking forward to a great reunion one of these days that will make up, by far, for the time that we were left behind.

Of course, to have this hope, you have to have faith in Jesus Christ—that He is God in the flesh, was born of a virgin, died for our sins and was raised again on the third day. If Jesus had not suffered and died this way, we, and especially me, wouldn't have this hope for tomorrow, because none of us could ever be good enough to get into heaven on our own.

Jesus said, according to John 14:1-4, "Let not your heart be troubled: ye believe in God, believe also in me. In my Father's house are many mansions: if *it were* not *so*, I would have told you. I go to prepare a place for you. And if I go and prepare a place for you, I will come again and receive you unto myself, that where I am, *there* ye may be also. And whither I go ye know, and the way ye know."[10]

A promise like that can't be beat. What more could you ask for?

Changes in the Landscape

The dog leg in the road is gone and the railroad crossing has been moved closer to the old Harlow's store to make a straight shot through Madison Run. The cars really whizz by at excessive speeds now. Also, they have started widening the road on up Dobyn's hill and on down towards Mallory's Ford.

Uncle Sam and Aunt Thomasia's house has been sold to some other people. The new owners covered the outside with vinyl, which really improved the looks of the place. They also remodeled the kitchen and bath. In addition, they re-plumbed and re-wired to some extent, but the front porch and yard could use a little looking after.

I wish that we could have bought the house ourselves. We had talked about how it could be fixed up to really look good. The Wood family just fixed up an identical house over near Lee's crossing and it looks great. At Christmas time it looks like one of those ceramic houses that are put on display.

I also thought about buying the old Roberts place, which joins both Aunt Thomasia's and the old Gipson place. It was for sale when I first started writing this section, but I decided that I did not want to go into debt so close to retirement.

Aunt Wilmeta's store has had a lot of work done to it. Vinyl siding has been added to the outside and the large rooms have been partitioned off to make more rooms, although I don't know how many. With just a few

---

[10] I have cited the King James version for this quote, but Gary's original man-uscript used a different version. —*Ed.*

finishing touches and some landscaping, that old store could really make someone a nice looking mansion.

There had been talk of putting a boot camp for troubled youths in Madison Run. It had already caused an uproar amongst the people down on the Moose Lodge road when they were talking about putting it down there, and the reaction was similar in Madison Run. One lady said that she didn't know why we were getting so upset, since there were just a bunch of junky, run-down houses around the neighborhood anyway. Even so, the neighborhood is our home.

I was at that lady's house a couple of years ago. At one point, she thought that I had left, and she was talking to someone in a very scornful manner about my house. She told the other person that "He ain't got nothin' but a couple of old fireplaces." Then her daughter rushed down to tell her that I was still there and it got quiet. I thought that was kind of funny. It didn't make me mad, though; it didn't even hurt my feelings.

A high pressure sewer line was built down the road on the track side one summer to serve a couple of factories near Aunt Virginia's place. For some reason, the people in charge of the county have decided that our area should be designated for industrial growth. I think more than anything else it's to keep the industrial area out of their own back yards.

1997

There are sad events that occur, and we know that they will occur, but we are never prepared for them. Just in the last ten years or so, it seems as if a lot of people are passing on who were rooted in Madison Run in some way or other.

The year 1997 saw the passing of Poochie Gipson, Lindsy Hall, Joe Cellars, Alton Hall, Louise Knighton and Tommy Grooms. As far as I can remember, the only one left of the older generation from out of town, who almost always comes back to Zion Baptist Church for home-coming day, is Buck Hicks.

Lindsy Hall came down with an illness while in Florida on vacation with his daughter Shirley. It turned out that he had terminal cancer. Lindsy always impressed me as being a pleasant gentleman, easy with a smile. Lindsy and Thomas (Buck) were brothers-in-law, since Lindsy was married to Buck's sister Dorothy. They lived next door to each other in the Richmond area for I think 50 years or so.

Shirley Frost called us before she left to winter in Florida to tell us that her Daddy had a tool chest in his shop that our Grandpop Allie had made for him many years ago. There was a 1936 calendar tacked inside it, so the chest was at least 62 years old at the time. Shirley said that if we wanted the chest we could have it, since our Grandpop Allie had built it.

Now, I'll have to say right here, not too many people would have been that thoughtful of others. Most would have just run it through an estate auction without saying anything about it. The thoughtfulness of Shirley and her family is greatly appreciated by all of our family (that is, the families of Ronnie and Gary Hogsten).

Since Shirley was going to be wintering in Florida for a couple of months, she left the key to Lindsy's shop with Buck. All we had to do was ride down to Richmond and Buck would give us the chest. This really worked out great because we had been planning to visit Buck any-way, and this inspired us to stop procrastinating and light out down the road. We hadn't been to see Aunt Charlotte in the nursing home for a while, either. While at the nursing home, we stopped in to see Nellie Hicks, Buck's sister in-law and, on the way home, we stopped to visit Earl Chandler at his country store.

Jackie and I had a great visit with Buck. It just so happened that his daughter Martha was there, also, and we had a good time looking at old pictures and trying to figure out who some of the people were in the old photographs.

We were unanimous in thinking that everyone should write on the backs of photographs the names of each individual pictured and the location, just in case it's an old home place or something. Who knows, maybe 70 years or so from now some people might be sitting around a table as we were, drinking a nice cup of coffee like the one Martha made for me, and puzzling amongst themselves, saying: "I wonder who this is? It looks sort of like Grandpop, or Grandma, or uncle, or aunt so and so...." And "Boy, they sure dressed funny back in those days!" And then they'll say "It sure would have been nice if someone would have taken the time to put names on all of these old pictures."

I expected the old chest to be really dinged and beat up, perhaps with broken or missing parts. But for a wooden tool chest that old, it really was in good condition, and it had just enough rash to give it a certain charm.

When I picked up the chest from Lindsy's shop, I stood there and looked around for a minute or two, noticing how everything was arranged. It had a certain neatness, but not so neat that it was just there to look at. It had an old-timey, useful look, like a place where many pleasant hours had been spent in days gone by, doing odd repairs on different things or maybe just tinkering to be tinkering—maybe just a little get away in the backyard.

I imagine that Lindsy and Buck, since they lived so close, probably got together in that little workshop and, while figuring out some major project, discussed and pondered many situations and circumstances over the years. Of course, that is what I like to imagine, and I can't help but think that I'm right.

Mr. Hall (Alton or "Papa") was really faithful in going to visit his wife Nellie in the nursing home for a couple of hours each day.

About the only time that he didn't make the visit was when he was sick or when the ground was covered with ice or snow.

As Mr. Hall was getting ready to go to the nursing home to see Nellie, he fell in his yard and broke his hip. After staying in the hospital for several weeks, he came home. After a couple of days, however, the repair job gave way. After a few more days in the hospital, he had to go to the Orange nursing home. I guess the only good thing about that was that he was in the same room as Nellie.

One day, Nellie Gray said, "I want to go home."

Papa told her "We *are* home, Mama."

While in the hospital, Mr. Hall said that he would like to be at home when he dies, but his condition made that almost out of the question. Still, Mr. Hall had been able to stay in his home longer than most people in his frail condition could have, probably because his daughter Ann fixed meals and kept a close check on him several times a day.

My daughter Becky went by the nursing home to visit Papa and Nellie one day and Papa said, "We have a visitor."

Nellie asked, "Who is it?"

Papa said, "It's Becky."

Nellie cocked her eye up a little bit and asked, "Hogsten?"

Becky's and Papa's birthdays were the same day and he always made note of that. In fact, when I came back from the hospital after Becky was born, the first place that I stopped was Zion church. Mr. Hall was there and was the first person that I told. I didn't know it was his birthday, too.

On those occasions when I stopped by for a visit with Papa, it was really enjoyable to hear stories about his growing up, the adventures he had with his siblings, how he came to live in Madison Run, how he lived in the little railroad tool house across from Harlow's store, and how he eventually bought the old Clea Bell house right at the railroad crossing. I really regret not getting around to taking a little day trip to Beaverdam with Papa, as we had planned to do, so that he could show us his old stomping grounds. It crossed my mind to tape record or even video tape conversations with Papa or other elderly people, but that would take the spontaneity away. It's better to let stories just flow into one's thoughts rather than sit there and try to think of a story to tell.

Mr Hall's little white house sure looks lonely sitting there, now that Papa has passed on.

Poochie Gipson passed on in February 1997. Poochie was one of the more colorful personalities born and raised in Madison Run. He was well known around the area for his horse and mule trading, fighting chickens, hunting dogs and his prowess as a hunter. For several years he owned a bulldozer and had an earth moving business. He also did a lot of cattle hauling around the country.

During the last several years of his life, Poochie was troubled with cancer and a stroke. I never did get to talk to him about his teenage years or ask him if the story was true about him having his feet tied together under a horse so that he couldn't be bucked off.

We rode through the cemetery the other day and saw the tombstone that was placed on Poochie's grave site. It really is a fitting monument for him. The stone is shiny black with scenes of a farm house and barn in the back ground, and two mules and four old hound dogs in the foreground. The etching on the stone has turned white, so the scenes really show up well.

Louise Knighton died, too. She and Kasandra Knicholson were the first Sunday school teachers at Zion church for me, Ronnie, Joyce, Peter, James, Alberta, William, Pokey, Carolyn, Wiggly, Judy, and a whole bunch of others whose names I can't remember right off. Louise always called Gary and Ronnie her boys, and she wanted us to be her pallbearers.

Another older buddy, Elwood Brockman, had a couple of heart attacks in a short time and then had to have an emergency operation to take out 12 or 14 inches of intestines that had gotten fouled up some way or other. And that was down right serious business for someone almost 90 years old. (Mr. Hall and Mr. Brockman were within about 4 days of being the same age, but Mr. Brockman always looked like he was right much stronger health wise, at least in the last couple of years.)

On a visit the day after his operation, Jackie patted Mr. Brockman's hand and told him "I'm so sorry that you have been so sick as of late."

He looked up at her and said, "You ain't half as sorry as I am."

That's pretty good wit for someone almost 90 and full of stitches.

Just a few months before his health crisis, Mr. Brockman came up to our house over on Route 647 and took down a huge dog pen that a girl who had been renting the house had left behind. That pen must have been 50 feet on a side, had 2-by-4s top and bottom nailed between each post, and had at least a thousand staples to pull that were holding the wire on.

I had put off doing that chore myself because it involved too much work; in fact, I was kind of dreading it. Mr. B. had it done in no time at all, and that sure was neighborly. It's supposed to be the other way around: the younger folk are supposed to do things for the older folk. Walking for exercise and keeping active were probably what helped Mr. Brockman pull through his health crisis, and he seems to be improving all the time.

Zion Baptist Church

On July 4th, 1997, we had the annual Zion Baptist church-wide cook-out at the old Gipson place.[11] With both regulars and visitors, there was a very good turn out. I had gotten a little behind in my mowing, so my nephew stopped by with one of his hot rod mowers. My nephew has a professional job in Charlottesville, but he also owns

---

[11] By this time, Gary had purchased the old Gipson place. —*Ed.*

his own lawn care business. Almost in the time that it takes me to get my old "Jim" and "Lulu" mowers gassed, greased and oiled, he had finished the free job and gone on to a paying one. As I said, there was a real good crowd on hand and everyone had a great time eating and talking.

Now someone, somehow, had acquired fireworks—possibly while on a trip to the Carolinas—to shoot off after dark. So, a fellow named Mike took the bush hog over on the other hill to mow off a 100-foot circle to have a safe place to fire everything off. Mike and another fellow named Bubba volunteered to shoot them off. I'll have to say, Bubba and Mike outdid themselves that time. It was the most beautiful fireworks display ever set off in Madison Run and the earth shook when those quarter sticks were set off. And you know, fireworks just aren't fireworks if they don't make a little noise once in a while.

After about an hour or so of the pyrotechnics display, someone commented on how safe an operation it had been since it had been done 400 feet or so from the crowd and there were only two people working in the firing area. Since they were about done, a fireman friend said his good-byes and started to leave, but Mike hollered from over on the hill "Don't leave yet."

So everyone got ready for the grand finale and we waited, and waited. Every once in a while we could see a spark flash, but nothing else. Finally, there was this blue flash and a thunderous ka-blooom—one of those explosions that you can feel. I thought to myself "Boy, that thing sure went off close to the ground!" In fact, it looked to me like it went off right where Bubba and Mike would have been standing. After a time, since no one had hollered from over on the hill, we figured that everything was all right.

So again our fireman friend starts to leave, but Mike yells out "Don't leave yet! We need some help over here. And bring a first-aid kit."

Since Mike was doing all of the yelling, I thought to myself, "Poor ol' Bubba must have gotten blown up and isn't able to say anything."

Since it was pitch black dark, we couldn't see what in the world was going on over at the firing site. The fireman said that he didn't have a kit, but I had one in my truck. So with fear, dread, and a sick, heavy-hearted feeling of what we would find over on the hill (and you can just imagine what was going through the mind of Bubba's wife), I jumped in the truck and tore out across the field. I fully expected poor ol' Bubba to be laid out on the ground, totally incapacitated, with maybe a body part or two separated, at least from his extremities, or maybe even worse. After all, that was a pretty powerful explosion that had gone off.

Upon arriving at the site where the fireworks were being set off, I pointed the headlights on the scene. Lo and behold, there was Bubba standing all in one piece, and there was Mike bent way over with his back to us and kind of leaning against Bubba and the truck. Immediately, the thought struck us that poor ol' Mike must be the one that had gotten blown up, maybe missing fingers, hands or even blinded. All kinds of stressful thoughts run through one's mind in a situation like that.

Someone hollered, "What's wrong!?"

Bubba said, "Mike has broken his arm."

By that time, we could see that everything was still attached and, glory be, he still had both eyes. We had almost gotten so that we could breathe again, and someone asked Bubba what had happened, since neither one of them had gotten blown up.

Bubba explained that the bow and arrow had backfired on Mike. Well, I've heard of gun barrels getting plugged and blowing up, and automobile engines backfiring through the mufflers, but that was a new one on me. A bow and arrow backfiring?

What had happened was that Mike had gone home and gotten his bow with the intention of tying a quarter stick on an arrow and shooting it up into the night time sky to have a spectacularly awesome, community-engulfing flash and explosion. (They say that a quarter stick is equivalent to one-fourth of a stick of dynamite and could be extremely dangerous if not handled in a proper manner.)

After tying the quarter stick to the arrow shaft, Mike drew his bow and waited for Bubba to light the fuse, and that's what that little spark was that we had seen over on the hill. But with Mike straining to hold the bow back, every time Bubba started to light the fuse, the match went out.

As you can imagine, by the time that ol' match had spluttered and went out a few times, and what with Mike being under all of that strain holding the bow drawn back with a quarter stick of dynamite 18 inches from his face, when that fuse did flare up, the pressure and strain on his nerves had become too great. Now, we all know that when you light the fuse on a regular firecracker you have the tendency to have a nervous jerk reaction when the fuse sparks up, so the only thing we could figure was that Mike accidentally let go of the bow instead of the string, and it came back and struck his arm.

When that thing, and I say this guardedly, "backfired," ol' Mike hollered "Run, Bubba!" and both of them lit out running because neither of them had any idea which way that bomb had gone. They just knew that it was still on the ground somewhere and the best thing to do was vacate the immediate vicinity.

It actually went off under the back end of Mike's truck and didn't do any damage that we could see. It wasn't until after the detonation, and after they had started back to the truck, that Mike came to realize that he had an injury to his arm, because by that time it had started to swell and throb a little.

Mike was really suffering with his arm. There was a big lump on the inside of the forearm that looked as if the bone was really out of line. Brenda said "I better go home and get the car to take Mike to the hospital," even though some of us had volunteered to do it. So we waited and waited, and waited some more, and all the while poor ol' Mike was really suffering with that arm. I guess thinking it was broken made it hurt even worse. At one point, when a little sweat ran down his arm, we even thought it had started to bleed. But Mike still wanted to wait for Brenda to get back. Finally, Ronnie got him in the car and took off to the hospital in Charlottesville, where Brenda later caught up with us.

It turned out that Mike's arm wasn't broken, but was bruised pretty badly, and he had to carry it in a sling for a week or so. We also found out that the reason Brenda had taken so long to get back with the car was because she figured, as long as she was at home, the dogs ought to be let out for a couple of minutes!

After it was all over and we found out Mike's arm wasn't broken, that evening's mishap turned out to be one of the most memorable, laughable, knee-slapping, Independence Day stories in Madison Run history. It still brings forth a chuckle now and then.

I'll have to say that it really wasn't all that funny at the time it happened. And I'm really not sure that Mike's arm wasn't injured by Bubba trying to get away from that bomb before it went off. It was one of those every-man-for-himself situations, after all, and we just missed having the July 5th news headlines read: "Senior citizen, chairman of the deacons at Zion Baptist church, blows self up playing with fireworks."

I must say that Zion church has been blessed with a multitude of powerful cooks over the years, even back in the good old days. At least I think they were the good old days, when there wasn't any running water or even a well at Zion; there were his and her cabins with new moons cut in the doors for restrooms; and homecoming meals were held outside. Long boards were nailed between trees to hold the food and they sagged with the bounty set before us all.

The only trouble was that all of the food sat outside on the board tables, and us little folks could look out of the open windows and see all of that food sitting there. Once in a while, a wonderful aroma would come wafting through the open windows. Shucks, that old preacher may as well have been howling at the moon as far as us little folks were concerned. He would have to have been preaching one squalling, howling, fired up sermon to have kept our attention off of that waiting banquet. It seemed to us like he was going to preach forever.

By 1992, I guess we were feeling a little smug in that we had a great, loving church that had no problems other than minor individual disagreements among the members. We had the reputation of having great fellowship, some of the best preaching that anyone could hear and members who welcomed visitors and new members into the fellowship.

One day when we were all sitting there, all snug and secure in our little world, someone came in and left a little crack in the door, through which old Satan must have slipped in, sat down among the flock and whispered in a few ears. It was just enough to start a little discord and dissension, to stir things up and cause a few hard feelings here and there among the flock. It seems as if the old Devil was pretty successful without having to waste a lot of his own energy.

In just the shortest amount of time, the church had split into three groups, two of which were solidly against each other and one smaller group that was sort of in the middle. We can blame it on the preacher, the school, the music program or anything else if we want to but, in the end, we each should accept a little of the responsibility ourselves. It is hard not to think that there was demonic influence in the break-up of a group of people who love the Lord and love each other. Some of us have known each other almost a lifetime, and some of us are even kinfolk. I think that I can say for me and everyone else at Zion, that all of the people who left are missed, and there is an empty spot in our lives at Zion Church.

We got a new preacher at Zion the first of October 1998. It's a little strange getting a preacher who is younger than a lot of us, especially when he's not but a year or so older than our children. Shucks, preachers are supposed to be the old fuddy-duddies, not us.

We were practicing a song at the church one night—"we" being me, Ronnie, Joe, and John (the new preacher)—when we got to talking about the building and how old it was.[12] Then the discussion got around to the addition that had been put on the back some years ago.

I told the others that at one point when the addition was being added, I was down in the hole dug out for the basement. While down there, I noticed something sticking out of the side of the hole that looked like the end of a bone. It turned out to be a casket handle. Looking a little closer, I saw the outline of a casket. The casket had been a wooden one and over the years it had rotted away. All that was left was a dark outline of one end. I don't know for sure, but I think the rest of that casket and some others might have been dug up and dumped in the fill dirt.

Then Ronnie mentioned the time when, as children, Joe and Charlie were hiding out from Amanda and Brandon in the basement of the church. They were crouched down, hiding in the same room with the

---

[12] The original portion of the main sanctuary of Zion Baptist Church was built before the Civil War, in 1858. During the war, the church building was reportedly used as a shoe factory for the Confederacy. This has spurred jokes about the ghosts of shoeless Confederate soldiers haunting the place. As an organization, Zion Baptist actually pre-dates its antebellum sanctuary, having started out in another building in 1813. —*Ed.*

wall that was against the spot where the casket had been dug up. The way the kids told it, there was a small table right at that spot. As they were hiding there, the table started to rattle and shake and then levitated off the floor. With fear in their hearts, Joe and Charlie did a triple time retreat from the basement. I guess they decided real quick that they were not going to hang around and see who or what might be shaking and picking up that ol' table.[13]

Come to think of it, me, Jackie, Jim and Pokey were over at the church painting the basement one night when we heard footsteps walking down the hall right above us. Me and Jim went straight upstairs to see who it was but, to our surprise, no one was there. All of the lights were off and no cars were outside. That was strange.

On the Road

On January 30th, 1998, at about 6:30 a.m., me and Jackie, who always rides shotgun, lit out down the road for our weekly Saturday morning ritual of going out for a cup of coffee and a biscuit, and then taking a little ride to who knows where. Upon arriving at Gordonsville, we went around the circle and headed up Rt. 33 towards Barboursville. We hadn't gone very far when Jackie asks me, where are we going? I really didn't know, so I turned ol' blue around and headed back to the

---

[13] Gary's nephew, Joe Hogsten, who is now an adult, confirmed to me that he and Charlie witnessed a bizarre incident as a child, probably in the late 1970s or early 1980s. According to Joe, he and Charlie were hiding in the basement of the church when they heard footsteps coming down the stairs and across the basement floor, but they saw no one. Then they heard a strange noise and a collection plate began to shake and rattle. Then the collection plate levitated off of the table and into the air. (So it was the plate, not the table, that levitated.) When I pressed him about the validity of this story, Joe insisted that he was very serious and not pulling my leg. —*Ed.*

traffic circle in Gordonsville. We stopped at the Tastee Freeze and got our coffee and biscuits there.

While sipping and munching, we headed out in a different direction, up Rt. 231, towards Rt. 250. After a couple of miles, my biscuit was gone and I still had a right goodly piece of coffee left in my cup (we always get large ones). Then the powerful urge came over me that I just had to have a doughnut, and not just any old grocery store doughnut, but a good old bakery doughnut, right out of the oven.

There was a doughnut store right on Rt. 250, just as you go into Charlottesville, right in the direction we were headed in. Shucks, what's another 15 miles, especially when a fellow gets the urge to have a nice custard-filled, chocolate-coated doughnut to eat with his coffee. And, as they say, I was chomping at the bit.

Well, you can imagine the let down when, upon arriving at the shop, it was closed.

But all was not lost. I'm not a quitter when it comes to the pursuit of a nice fresh doughnut. My mind was set. The situation called for perseverance, so after another 20 minute ride across the city of Charlottesville, we hit the jackpot. One dozen doughnuts: six Bavarian creme, six plain glazed, and one large coffee to warm up the ones we already had.

I tell ya, it will be a sad day when that old diabetes that runs in the family catches up with me and I won't be able to indulge in such sweet delicacies. Of course, clogged arteries could be a nuisance, too.

Jackie reminded me of this when she said, "You shouldn't be eating all of that junk." I did happen to notice, though, as we were heading down the highway towards Zion Crossroads, that there were five doughnuts missing from the box, and I only remember eating two.

After driving almost to Richmond, we turned around and came up Rt. 522 near Darnita's parents' home. By the way, Darnita, after all of these years of being family, still won't agree with me no matter what the subject. I guess she can't stand to be wrong.

After making a circuit down through a lot of back roads, through the communities of Buckner, Bumpass, Fredricks Hall, Mineral, Louisa, and Peck's store, we finally ended up at the back entrance of Blue Ridge Shores, which is where Joyce Palmer lives. After a little visit with Joyce and Kenneth, we headed on out through the piney woods, across where Mallory's Ford should still be instead of that ugly bridge, through the Cox's Mill crossroads, up by the Knights, and on over the crest of Dobyn's hill, from where a person can see a panoramic vista of Madison Run, and on down to the old Gipson place, which is home.

So ended a 200-mile jaunt in our old, blue-gray, primer spotted, wheezing, knocking, smoking, '78 Chevrolet truck. Ronnie says that one day he expects to get a call from us from some far-off location to come and give us a ride home.

But anyway, wadda ya know, there are still some doughnuts left. Sunday morning breakfast.

We were coming home one night after listening to a gospel music concert in Fredericksburg and stopped at a convenience store for a snack. I purchased a big old wiener sausage. As I was putting mustard on the thing, it rolled off of the bun and onto the floor. So automatically I stuck my foot out to break the fall, which was almost like a mini drop kick. The wiener sausage went rolling across the floor, and there was mustard on my freshly washed tennis shoe and all over the floor.

I asked the girl behind the counter if she had some place to wash that sausage off, because that would have been almost two dollars wasted. Instead, she gave me another and wrote that one off. (But I do wonder if she didn't wash it off later.) Anyway, everyone in the van got a good laugh out of the incident.

We had a church van full of people for the trip. Millie Miller was driving, Jim Snipes was riding shotgun, Thelma Lutz, Edith Atkins, Meredith Hall, Loraine Hall, Ronnie Hogsten, Nancy Embree, Jackie Hogsten, Darnita Hogsten, Jennifer Hogsten and I were all in the back. The music was great, but I think the best part of the trip was the fellowship we all had together, just talking and laughing.

After parting with everyone back at the church, Jackie and I started home. As we got near Mr. Hall's house and the Perkins' house, Neil Lutz's big, old black dog charged out into the road. I only saw him for an instant and didn't have time to even touch the brakes. Both driver's side wheels ran over him, but the poor old dog made it home before he died.

We weren't going but about 20 miles per hour. Probably if I had been going a little faster, the old dog wouldn't have been able to get in front of the wheels. He would have fell in behind.

I guess being night time, the old dog misjudged his speed and distance. I hate to run over a woolly worm in the road, must less someone's pet dog.

On the Job

At the risk of sounding like I'm writing a diary, I'm going to say that I'm sitting here at Melton, right on the other side of the tracks, on the old dirt road that used to be the original road between Louisa and Gordonsville before they built Route 33. It's pouring down a cold, icy rain and I am sitting here in my telephone truck, waiting for it to slack up long enough so that I can get my tent up without getting too wet. I tell ya, a po' ol' telephone cable splicer sure has a miserable job when there is a cold precipitation falling down—even worse when there is a lot of mud. And there is always lots of sticky, nasty mud. Most every job I get to splice up, the contractors have just put the cable in the ground, so it is always like walking in a wet, freshly plowed garden.

Rain or not, I'm going to have to get out very shortly because, as the old saying goes, my eyeballs are almost floating. I guess that's kind of crude, but it's the truth.

On the Farm

Well, it's the first day of October 1998, 10:30 a.m. I have just come inside after putting the finishing touches on my old 8N Ford tractor and then making a few passes around the field, with the bush hog roaring and grinding behind me.

The project with the old tractor started back in April when it came to me that I ought to replace the axle pin and bushing in the front end, because every time I installed a new distributor cap the axle would come up too far and break it. Then it would only run on three cylinders and, since it only has four to start with, dragging that dead piston up and down probably cut the power back to about half. Anyway, after about two years of fretting with the thing, I finally resolved to do something about it.

The problem is that every time I start what to me is a small project, it almost always ends up being a major operation. And so it was with the tractor project.

I'll say to myself, heck, as long as I've got this loose I might as well do that, too, and since I'm doing that I might as well do another thing. And so it goes, pyramiding upward till I'm in up to my nose in a minor project that has turned out to be a major one. Then I think to myself, why didn't I just leave well enough alone? It really wasn't all that bad to start with, and at least it was working.

The way the 8N project started was that we had bought 12 acres with an old, seriously rundown house on it, built circa 1850. My Grandma's brother, Uncle Tom, owned it before 1900 and lived there with his wife and 11 children until about 1927. Then my Mama's first cousin, Uncle

Tom's daughter, and her husband bought it. Along with their 10 children, they lived there until 1961 and 1964, respectively, when they passed on. Then my Uncle Sam bought it to do a little weekend farming on. When he died in 1976, it was passed to his children—my first cousins—whom we bought the place from in 1988.

The place was always called a little farm and, in the past, a good part of the families' living was earned off of it—mainly pigs, chickens, milk cows, and a strong vegetable garden. The property also adjoined that of my home place. Its pasture was the neighborhood playing field for football, baseball, soccer, rasselin' (I know it's wrestling), cowboys and Indians, hide and seek, or just stomping around in the spring water.

But anyway, we ended up owning the place and needed a tractor to do a lot of clearing and other work. A coworker of mine said that his brother had a tractor for sale for $1500 but that I probably could get it for $1300. Well, it turned out to be $1500, but a front end loader came with it. It came with an old rake, too, but I've never gone back to get it. That front end loader by itself turned out to be worth a whole lot more than what I paid for the tractor. It was really a surprise to me what could be done with it.

Well, back to the 8N project. After pulling the hood off to get to the axle pin and bushing, I found that the type of pin that was needed for the front end loader was no longer available from Ford or the other local suppliers. That called for cutting the front end loader mounting plate off of the old pin and welding it on to the new one. I had to pay $47 for welding, since I no longer have access to a welder myself. Then I had to put a new spline disc on the end of the crankshaft that drives the pump shaft, since the other one got walloped out while running at too high a speed while bush-hogging. I had been removing the shaft and propping the loader up while bush-hogging, but I got lazy a couple of times and it cost me time and money.

One of the radius rods was bowed up, but after I set a six-ton jack between the rod and an 8-by-8 timber, and chained the ends down, it straightened out nicely. Then I thought to myself, since I've gone this far, it wouldn't be that much more trouble to paint the whole tractor.

Some way or other a stick got stuck between the rim and tire on the front. Since the tire had to come off anyway, I went on and had both front tires pulled off the rims, which made it easier to paint them. The rear tires I just rolled back, propped up, and masked with tape and paper. Wouldn't you know, after standing there propped up for a week, as soon as the last coat of paint was applied, one of the tires fell over. It went "whoosh!" and all of that dry dirt and grass really made a mess to have to clean off of that fresh paint.

After pulling the fenders and wheels off, I finally got around to checking on why the right rear brake had never worked in the ten years that I had owned the N. The asbestos pad had come off of the shoe completely and was just laying in there in pieces. The rest of the brakes on the N were like new, so I went to the local New Holland dealer. After a little searching, the parts man came up with a shoe set that someone had used half of, so he sold me the other half for $14, and I was grateful.

After spraying on about ten cans of Gunk, with lots of scraping and hosing between each can, and then washing it down with three gallons of some kind of detergent from NAPA auto supply using a sprayer with 120 lbs. of air pressure, the fuselage was ready for paint. I had bought a cheap spray gun to use for spraying primer to save wear on my good gun, so I thought to myself, why not use it to spray on this implement paint? Well, it turned out that the cheap gun sprays by pressurizing the cup with about 30 lbs. of pressure. Not thinking, I plugged it in with the regulator set at 120 lbs. Needless to say, the fully filled cup blew off with a pop. Other than painting my shoes, a nearby jack and the surrounding grass red, not much damage was done.

After that lesson was learned, and I was into about the third coat of paint on the fuselage, I got to messing with the spray adjustment on back of the spray gun, trying to get a little more paint to come out of the gun. For some reason, about the time I started to spray again, the adjustment screw came all the way out. Since the paint cup is pressurized, and since the screw is on the back of the gun and the back of the gun is aimed at whoever is using it, and since I am right handed, in an instant the right side of my body changed in hue, including my hair.

What a mess. By the time I got through with that red paint, the ground where I was working looked as if there had been a massacre or something, and I could have passed for a badly wounded survivor. I tell you, in trying times like that, it's kind of hard not to utter some very un-Christian-like phrases—especially when you have sticky red paint dripping from your eyebrows.

After getting all of the tractor painted, I put in a new wire harness, plugs, plug wires, points, condenser, coil, amp, oil gauges, radiator pad, distributor cap, Ford emblem on the hood, and some other doodads. When everything was reassembled, we went out for a little buzz around the field pulling the bush hog.

About halfway around the field, there was this tree limb hanging down, under which I had driven many times before and had just let the limbs slide across the hood. Before, there had always been old, hard, rusty paint, but this time there was new soft paint.

One scratch on the front of the hood was about six inches, and another one along side the gas tank door was about eight inches and cut down to the primer. There were also long brown scrapes the length of the hood. It was enough to cause me to start thinking about those phrases again.

After rubbing down the damaged areas with some paint thinner to get the marks off and soften up the edges of the scratches, and a little deft work with a foam brush, it now takes a good eye to see where the damage was done. You expect a tractor to get scratched and dinged over time, but it's kind of upsetting to have it happen that soon after looking so pretty.

The bush hog itself was also in dire need of a paint job. Since I had some paint left over, it seemed like a good idea to spray some on. About halfway through, the paint ran out, so it was back to Culpeper (a 50-mile round trip) to get another gallon. Then I thought to myself, since I'm going to have paint left over after the second gallon, shucks, I might as well paint the front end loader, too. And since I'm doing that, I might as well throw a coat on the three-point hitch boom. And, come to think of it, that old disc I bought the other day for $25 could use some paint, too. And I almost forgot, the three-point hitch truck needs paint. Come to think of it, the Troy-built tiller needs paint and it's red, too.

Boy, putting an axle pin in a 8N Ford tractor sure turns out to be a lot of work!

"Jim" is an old Sears Craftsman riding lawn mower that Pastor Jim Burks gave me. He suggested that it would be good for dragging or pulling stuff around the place, even though it could no longer be used to cut grass.

Being that I'm my father's son, however, when that old lawn mower fired right up and purred right along just as pretty as you please, a brilliant idea hit me. I thought to myself, "this thing runs so good, why not get a mower deck and put this thing into operation?" After all, I can always use another good mower and, man-o-man, this one has 16 horsepower! That would really be moving up in horses over my old 12 and 8 horsepower mowers.

So the search began for a used deck, since the cost for a new one would be out of sight. After two weeks, I located one in another town for $100, take it or leave it. Well, I took it, even though it was a bit on the rusty side. After all, what's a little rust? A little paint would take care of that.

Did I say a *little* paint? I don't know if you would call four cans of Rustoleum and four cans of Dollar General paint a little or not, at around 22 bucks (back then).

Well, finally! After all the painting, the deck is mounted and cutting grass. Whoops. What's that? Sounds like there's some trouble in the transmission. Yup. The gears are chipped up, causing some slippage; probably needs a shim to tighten the gears up a little.

After a tear-down, though, it is obvious that a shim is not going to do it. It's going to need a couple of gears. A "couple" turns out, by the way, to be 7 gears, 18 bearings, 6 seals, an axle shaft, a main power shaft, a giant drive pulley, 5 pounds of grease and an assortment of shims and clips.

So, the next day, I'm off to Sears to order parts. What's that? Three-hundred dollars? Goodness! Well, I am already in the hole $122 for the deck—might as well fix it right. Since it's going to take 30 days to get the transmission parts, I might as well spray a little paint on the rest of the mower. This calls for three evenings of sanding, disassembly and preparation, plus six more cans of Rustoleum to the tune of about $25, followed by a day of replacing hood, fenders, dash, etc.

Then the parts start arriving. Trouble is, it took so long to get them, I've forgotten how they came out. After a time of trial and error, success! It all goes together.

Finally, payola. I'm humming along cutting grass. Man, this is a brute—money well spent. But wait—why is one side of the deck digging a furrow like a garden plow? Well, back to the place in the grass where I keep my tools. They are easy to find if the grass is kept cut down with the weed eater. A little rust won't hurt them; they are pretty thick metal. Besides, if I put them away, I never can find them.

After all kinds of trials and errors, I realized that it was going to take another trip to the mower junk yard to get a set of wheels to put on each side of the deck. Another $15.

Soon I'm cutting grass again and this thing is really doing a good job. Whoops. The blades quit. Must have been that old belt I used. Sixteen more bucks.

Back in business again, I'm really zipping along, whacking grass, and it's level, too. Whups. The thing has quit again. Another $16 belt down the tubes. Back to the tool storage area in the grass. This time it's a pulley. But this time I'm in luck. The old deck that came with the mower still had this part and a couple of others.

Finally, we're in business again and the grass is going down. Oops. What in the world is that awful noise? There goes the belt again. Back to Sears for more deck parts. The parts came pretty quickly but, because of an injurious fall on my part (probably because of the distraction caused by that stinking mower), it was eight months before I was in good enough shape to work on the dirtyrottenstinkingpieceofnogoodjunk.

So, after eight months, it's back to work on Jim Mower. I guess you could call that being a glutton for punishment.

I get the new parts out (that had been ordered eight months earlier) and I'm ready to get to work. The trouble is, the old parts won't come off. I need to use some of the old parts, but even after heating them with a torch, they won't come off. In a fit of rage, I proceed to remove said parts with a four pound hammer. Success! They come off. Trouble is, the parts that I need to re-use are the ones that broke.

I say to myself, in a scream that is loud enough to be heard all over Madison Run, "Why me?!" What kind of luck is it that nothing ever goes right, nothing ever works the way that it should? Oh, well. It just isn't my day—again.

Well, I finally got the new parts installed, but I still had to make another trip to the Sears store in Charlottesville for more new parts and I still had to use some parts off the old deck, too.[14] A few moans, groans, and tantrums later, and I'm back doing my thing. I mean, this mower is really slaying this tall grass. Man-oh-man, this thing is a brute—a really fine, motorized, grass-cutting machine.

---

[14] A car trip from Madison Run to Charlottesville, by the way, is more than 30 minutes one way. —*Ed*

Well, since Jim Mower runs and looks so good with that new paint job, maybe I should go on and get a new sealed beam to replace the broken one. So I special order a bulb at the cost of $11 and it won't even fit.

Eventually, though, I'm humming right along, cuttin' good, runnin' perfect—one mighty fine machine. Uh-oh, what's that bumping? It can't be! Two flat tires at the same time?

After the addition of the tires, a new $50 seat (the old one almost dumped me off when it broke), and another new $28 belt (a main drive one, this time), I started to think to myself that I might have to take out a bank loan to keep Jim Mower running. The fellow that designed the deck, by the way, must have already had that long belt on hand and didn't want to waste it. That belt zigs and zags, loops and turns, and doubles back along about eight different pulleys. It has to be seen to be believed. The guy must have learned his trade in a maze.

Later on, I had to pull the transmission out to adjust the gearshift, which called for taking off the fenders and the seat anyway, so it wasn't too much extra trouble to replace the belt. Trouble was, after the wheels, transmission, seat and some other stuff were all bolted back together, the new belt had come off, so another tear-down was needed. And that old cedar tree must have moved, because when I started I was in the shade.

The thing finally went back together and only one bolt got lost in the process. Also, I hacked and sawed a bigger notch in the gearshift slot so that it would go in reverse.

So, eventually, JM was running and cutting just fine, with plenty of power. A new mower probably could have been purchased for what I spent on JM, and that doesn't include the hypertension, band-aids and skin off my knuckles. I didn't have to plunk down a big pile of money for a new mower—I just paid for a "free" mower one piece at a time.

Now that I think about it, though, that mower was out to get me. It attacked me twice. Once, when I was standing beside it trying to get it started, the thing fired up, ran over my foot, and mowed down a nice little dogwood tree that Lulu had planted. A big old cedar finally put an end to the rampage. What really convinced me that I was in harms way, however, was the day that I left the motor running and parked it in neutral to go pick up a rock laying in the grass. When I look backed, Jim Mower was coming at me. I had just enough time to jump aside, then it ran down a pretty good sized oak tree that I had planted a while back. It just flattened the tree and stopped with its wheels sitting right on the trunk.

I don't really believe in evil lawn mowers, but Jim Burks did seem awfully happy when he unloaded that thing at my house. Makes me kind of wonder.

Now, if I can just get a new muffler ordered to replace the one that fell off in three pieces....

EPILOGUE

That's about it. I wrote this as honestly and sincerely as I could. Looking back, I feel like we had an enviable childhood, and I still say the pre-teen years were the best.

So I'll conclude with one last childhood memory. We had a book when we were little that had a picture of Resurrection Day. In this picture, the graves were open. Men, women and children were standing in and around the graves, smiling, and the sky was lit up with clouds rolling away on all sides.

One day, there was a great thunder storm with lightning and rain, and dark clouds all over. It was a dark and frightening storm, especially to little folks. We sat around real quiet till it was over, because Grandma had said that the Lord was at work and that we should not be making noise jumping around. The way that old storm was flashing lightning and thundering, with wind howling and rain beating down on our tin roof, we figured she must be right, because it would take a mighty power to cause all of that action.

Anyway, after the storm was over, we took a walk with Mama down the road. Although the sun was starting to break through in one part of the sky, we were still under dark clouds. It was sort of like being in a dark tunnel, and we were looking ahead, down the tracks, toward Aunt Virginia's. The fields and the sky were lit up like some giant spotlight was shining down. It was so pretty that I just don't have the words to describe it, other than to say that it reminded me of that picture of Resurrection Day, only the scene was even more brilliant than the picture.

It's hard to forget times like that. How dear to my heart are the scenes of my childhood, when fond memories present them to view!

APPENDIX A: THE MADISON RUN HALL OF FAME

In the introduction to this book, I wrote about the old people slipping away one at a time and, before we know it, they are all gone and we miss them. I know I sure do. I guess it's kind of ironic. They are up in heaven, just as happy as larks, and we are down here, all sad because they are gone. Of the many older folks whom our family looked on with love and fondness over the years, few are still alive. I wonder if our children and grandchildren will remember our generation as fondly as we remember our elders?

Carl McClendon: Great fisherman.

Bob Gipson and Virginia Atkins: Best gardeners.

Sylvia Hogsten: Zion Church piano player and great canner.

Peter and James Mundy: Drove horse-drawn sled to store and hanged Joyce.

Miss Eleanor:	Played with us on rock pile
Billy:	Out-drew Marshall Dillon and shot TV with pistol
William Hicks:	Could kick a football as far as a pro
Slick:	Best expectorator
Jeep:	Fastest runner
Ronnie:	Deadly aim throwing rocks
Gary (me):	Seller of seeds, cosmetics, plums and pot-holders; builder of model airplanes
Carolyn and Phyllis:	Great Jitterbug dancers
Aunt Charlotte:	Best seamstress
Joe Hogsten:	Cut hair at Rosa's store
Runt B. and Mush D.:	Rode belt-driven motorbikes in the neighborhood
Etna Estes:	Frowned on anyone fishing in her pond
Mary Agnes' husband; Jenny H.'s husband; and Mr. Wolfrey:	Killed by trains

Marvin:	Best football player and bike crasher
Dickie Mundy:	Had a Roman Candle back-fire down his shirt collar
John Bibb:	Had a hot '54 Oldsmobile and took us on drag race
Aubrey Seal:	Flipped a Model A Ford over near our house
Bob Gipson:	Slowest driver
Poochie:	Horse breaker
Mabel Gipson:	Fed the hungry
Grandma Rosa; Aunt Thomasia; and Aunt Wilmeta:	Witnessed about the Lord

APPENDIX B:
A MOTHER'S DEATH

This is a letter that I sent to Francis and Chester of Baltimore, Maryland. They were friends of Mama (Sylvia) and Daddy (Joe).

Dear Chester and Francis,

We received your Christmas card to Mama last Christmas, 1995, and were going to write back to you, but somehow the envelope with your address got lost. I was hoping that you would send another one this year, 1996, so that we could get your address and write back to you.

It was really nice to get a card from Mamas old friends. I have heard your names before but can't remember ever seeing you, probably because I haven't been on Holibird avenue since I was 4 years old, and that's been over 50 years.[15]

Mama died on the 9th of December 1991, about 7:00 p.m., just as she, my wife Jackie and my mother in-law were getting ready to go visit

---

[15] Those readers who are familiar with Baltimore might notice the misspelling of Holabird Avenue. Given the sensitive and heartfelt nature of this letter, I thought that it would be best to leave Gary's original text unaltered. —*Ed.*

a home for the retarded and outcasts to help with a Christmas program. Mama was to play the piano for the singing.

She passed on with a good deed in her heart, and she passed without having to go through the infirmities that sometimes come with getting older, so I guess we are selfish for wishing she were still here.

Mama was loved and is missed by all.

Sincerely,

Gary Hogsten

Top left: Gary's mother, Sylvia, on the side porch of the old home place.

Top right: Gary and Ronnie on the tracks.

Bottom left: Gary's Grandma, dressed for church.

Bottom right: Gary, his father Joe, and Ronnie.

(Photos from author's personal collection.)

Above: The old home place (Gary's parents' house) provides the background for Gary and his bow.

Below: Bub, Ronnie and Slick in the driveway of the old home place, near the spot where two Confederate soldiers had once been buried.

(Photos from author's personal collection.)

Above: Gary's parents, Sylvia and Joe, surrounded by family.

Front row, left to right: Jack Mundy, Rosalee Grooms, Aileen Mundy, Annalee Grooms and Tommy Grooms.

Back row, left to right: Thomas Grooms, Rosa Hicks Mundy, Fanny Mundy Grooms, Allie Mundy, Sylvia Mundy Hogsten, Joe Hogsten, Margaret Mundy and Woodson Mundy.

(Photo from author's personal collection.)

Left: The train engine that struck and killed Mr. Wolfrey, probably in the late 1940s or early 1950s, suffered front end damage. *(Photo courtesy of R. Lutz.)*

Right: The oil stove of terror. *(Photo from author's personal collection.)*

Above: "Jim," the evil (?) lawn mower, was still functioning in 2002.

Below: The 8N Ford tractor was still looking good, too.

(Photos by Mark Burton.)

Above: The Zion Baptist Church building has undergone various renovations and additions since Gary was a child, but the original antebellum sanctuary is still used for services.

Below: The old home place (Gary's parents' house) as it appeared in 2002.

(Photos by Mark Burton.)

0-595-26539-1